Crocodile

Animal
Series editor: Jonathan Burt

Already published

Ant Charlotte Sleigh · *Ape* John Sorenson · *Bear* Robert E. Bieder
Bee Claire Preston · *Camel* Robert Irwin · *Cat* Katharine M. Rogers
Chicken Annie Potts · *Cockroach* Marion Copeland · *Cow* Hannah Velten
Crocodile Dan Wylie · *Crow* Boria Sax · *Dog* Susan McHugh
Donkey Jill Bough · *Duck* Victoria de Rijke · *Eel* Richard Schweid
Elephant Dan Wylie · *Falcon* Helen Macdonald · *Fly* Steven Connor
Fox Martin Wallen · *Frog* Charlotte Sleigh · *Giraffe* Edgar Williams
Hare Simon Carnell · *Horse* Elaine Walker · *Hyena* Mikita Brottman
Kangaroo John Simons · *Leech* Robert G. W. Kirk and Neil Pemberton
Lion Deirdre Jackson · *Lobster* Richard J. King · *Monkey* Desmond Morris
Moose Kevin Jackson · *Mosquito* Richard Jones · *Ostrich* Edgar Williams
Otter Daniel Allen · *Owl* Desmond Morris · *Oyster* Rebecca Stott
Parrot Paul Carter · *Peacock* Christine E. Jackson · *Penguin* Stephen Martin
Pig Brett Mizelle · *Pigeon* Barbara Allen · *Rat* Jonathan Burt
Rhinoceros Kelly Enright · *Salmon* Peter Coates · *Shark* Dean Crawford
Snail Peter Williams · *Snake* Drake Stutesman · *Sparrow* Kim Todd
Spider Katja and Sergiusz Michalski · *Swan* Peter Young · *Tiger* Susie Green
Tortoise Peter Young · *Trout* James Owen · *Vulture* Thom Van Dooren
Whale Joe Roman · *Wolf* Garry Marvin

Crocodile

Dan Wylie

REAKTION BOOKS

Published by
REAKTION BOOKS LTD
33 Great Sutton Street
London EC1V 0DX, UK
www.reaktionbooks.co.uk

First published 2013
Copyright © Dan Wylie

Printed and bound in China by C&C Offset Printing Co., Ltd

British Library Cataloguing in Publication Data
Wylie, Dan
    Crocodile. – (Animal)
    1. Crocodilians.
    I. Title II. Series
    597.9'8-DC23

ISBN 978 1 78023 087 0

Contents

1 The Survivor

The title of this book is misleading. It should really be *Crocodilian*, since it explores not only what are sometimes called 'true crocodiles', but the closely related species of alligators, caimans and gharials. The latter are not 'false crocodiles', but equally respectable members of the same family. Today there are at least 23 recognized crocodilian species, roaming the waters of the globe from Brazil to Bali, from Florida to Formosa, from the Congo to China. They have done so, in some or other shape, since before our familiar continents were even formed, since before the great extinction event some 65 million years ago that eradicated the dinosaurs. They are truly among the evolving Earth's most extraordinary survivors. Only now, as humans hunt them to the brink of extinction and destroy their habitats, are some crocodilian species beginning to be in serious danger of vanishing.

It doesn't help, of course, that they persist in eating people; many humans still regard their 'cold-blooded', predatory life-ways as excuse enough to vilify them, kill them, eat them, and turn them into handbags and shoes. If there is a single word most commonly associated with crocodiles, it is 'infested': crocodile habitats are described, with numbing regularity, as 'crocodile-*infested* waters'. Hugh Stayt wrote in 1968:

The appearance of the crocodile is so uncouth and repulsive and its method of attack so subtle and dangerous that it produces an attitude of repulsion and fear in the minds of all men. This attitude reacts either in the veneration and avoidance of the subject of fear, or in hate and antagonism, culminating in a passion for destroying the hated creature.[1]

Yet, surprisingly often, crocodilians have been worshipped, appealed to, represented and treasured, albeit almost always with a tinge of fearfulness. For tens of thousands of years, Africans, Australasian Aboriginals and early Americans incorporated reverence and propitiation of crocodilians into their animistic mythologies and rituals. Only more recently have the biblical, Cartesian and Kantian strains of Western philosophy desig-nated animals as merely tools for human use – with appalling consequences for them. Yet even in Europe, where crocodiles have not lived in the wild in human memory, there has been a counter-discourse. Porphyry of Tyre (234–c. 305 CE) suggested:

If we define, by utility, things which pertain to us, we shall not be prevented from admitting that *we* were generated for the sake of the most destructive animals, such as crocodiles.[2]

Even in our secular, technologized era, crocodilians remain an unsettling reminder of humans' natural vulnerability. We have used them deplorably, even as we newly appreciate their ecological importance. Hence an important theme of this book is human cultures' difficult, entangled progression from fear *of* crocodiles, to fear *for* them.

How *did* crocodilians survive so long, essentially unchanged?

Some clues can be found in their present-day physiology, so let's begin with the basic crocodilian body. Imagine you're standing on the bank of Rudyard Kipling's 'great grey-green greasy Limpopo' River in Africa, blissfully unaware of impending doom until . . . you spot, just breaking the water's surface, the bit that shows itself first: the nostrils. Crocodilians smell keenly: a whiff of potential prey in the water can attract them from hundreds of yards away. As the nostrils break the surface, nasal flaps open; air is sucked in with a characteristic 'sniff'. On submersion, the flaps close, preventing flooding of the nasal tubes. These run not into the oral cavity, but further back to a cup-shaped cavity behind the gular flap which seals the throat under water. Oddly,

A crocodile farm guide shows the gular flap at the back of the throat.

9

A sharp eye.

crocodilians lack Jacobson's organ, which in other reptiles detects scent molecules in the mouth itself.

Next to appear above the waterline are the raised but retractable lids of cartilage housing the eyes. The crocodilian eye is remarkably sharp, registering some colour. It is slitted like a cat's for maximum light-enhancement, helped by an extra layer of cells in the retina, the *tapetum lucidum*; this is what reflects light back from a torch at night. Do those expressionless eyes really exude tears, as the saying suggests? It is an idea laden with humans' projection onto the crocodile of their own vulnerability: attacking so surreptitiously, the crocodile embodies deceit. The pseudonymous compiler Sir John Mandeville in the four-teenth century, uncritically repeating a blend of medieval legend and Aristotle, asserted that 'cockodrills' were like 'serpents' that 'slay men, and they eat them weeping'. The crocodile is, as Edmund Spenser put it in *The Faerie Queene* (1590), a 'cruell craftie' monster

THEN AND NOW.—1862 AND 1882.

Crocodile tears over the fate of Jews from U.S. President Ulysses S. Grant, 1882.

"OH, NOW YOU WEEP, AND I PERCEIVE YOU FEEL
THE DINT OF PITY. THESE ARE GRACIOUS DROPS."

'Which, in false griefe hyding his harmefull guile / Doth weepe full sore, and sheddeth tender teares' (I.v.18). Similarly, Shakespeare's deceived hero Othello curses, 'Oh devil, devil! if that the earth could teem with woman's tears, / Each drop she falls would prove a crocodile' (IV.i). The crocodile *does* have tear ducts that excrete proteinaceous fluid to keep the third, nictitating

11

eyelid lubricated; if the crocodile is out of the water and dry for any length of time, leaking of moisture may be visible. But emotion plays no part – any more than it does in that strange consequence among humans of Bell's palsy, also called Bogorad's or 'crocodile tears syndrome', whose sufferers weep uncontrollably while eating.

Just behind the crocodile's eyes, flaps of skin cover oblong ear openings. Crocodilian hearing is also excellent, detecting sounds from 100 to 4,000 hertz (cycles per second), possibly enhanced by the auditory canal running across the front of the skull. Crocodilians listen to one another. Uniquely among reptiles some, notably American alligators, emit 'roars' or bellows, audible for up to 150 m and sometimes preceded by infrasonic (low-frequency) underwater reverberation. Observers differ on whether roaring is sexual or territorial; the early Florida traveller and naturalist William Bartram claimed they responded to thunder, and crocodile managers in South Carolina told me the creatures react to passing trucks. They can hear humans, too, some of whom have purportedly made a career of 'calling crocodiles'. A central African Nyanza legend tells of a fugitive prince named Bukango who finds that, 'with a strange *hooing* sound' like a flute, he can call on the crocodiles to bring him fish while fleeing his tyrannical uncle, and to protect him when he elopes with his girl.[3]

Not only has your predator smelt, seen and heard you; it has *felt* you irreverently paddling in the shallows. Crocodilians are unique in possessing, along the face in particular, small pits in the skin that are fantastically sensitive to disturbances in the water. The pits, or dermal pressure receptors (DPRS), attach to an exceptionally thick trigeminal cranial nerve, and respond to ripples emanating from a single drop of water. They are more sensitive than human lips.[4] As the crocodile rises further towards you, its massive skull becomes visible. It houses a bird-like brain

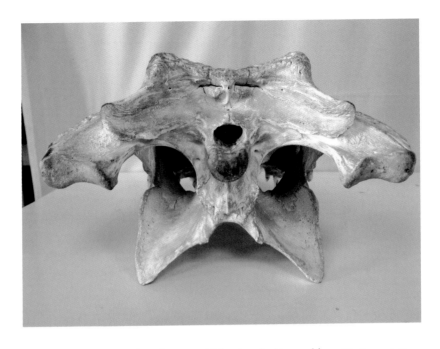

that is not much larger than the proverbial walnut but is capable of surprising intelligence.

Then the most fearsome article of all: the long, yawning jaw, with its yellowy pink interior and its rows of between 60 and 110 interlocking teeth. Conical, pointed and designed to grip and puncture, not to chew, these teeth are shed and replaced alternately throughout the animal's life, up to 50 times. Before you are gripped, crushed, dragged under and torn apart, you'll have barely a second to recall that the teeth are talismans of magical power in many cultures; or you might remember the tale that certain birds have the temerity to pick morsels from between them as the crocodile basks with its mouth open. Aristotle called the bird the 'trochilus' – usually identified as a plover – which thereby

The heavy skull, showing the tiny cavity that houses the brain.

gets his food, and the crocodile gets ease and comfort; it makes no attempt to injure its little friend, but, when it wants it to go, it shakes its neck in warning, lest it should accidentally bite the bird.[5]

Even more fantastically, in the seventeenth century English playwright John Webster depicted in *The White Devil* how the crocodile, 'that the bird may not talk largely of her abroad for non-payment, closeth her chaps, intend[ing] to swallow her'. However, 'nature, loathing such ingratitude, hath armed this bird with a quill or prick on the head, top o' th' which wounds the crocodile i' th' mouth, [and] forceth her open her bloody prison'. The name 'trochilus' stuck at least into the nineteenth century, when Thomas Lovell Beddoes fancifully wrote in his poem 'A Crocodile' how

In the iron jaws
Of the great devil-beast, like a pale soul
Fluttering in rocky hell, lightsomely flew
A snowy trochilus, with roseate beak
Tearing the hairy leeches from his throat.

There is actually neither hellish nor pleasant symbiosis between reptile and bird, though sundry observers insist they have spotted some opportunistic dental flossing by plovers or wagtails.

So awesomely relaxed when agape in hot sun – possibly part of their complex heat-regulation mechanism – those jaws, utiliz - ing 120-odd muscles, exert huge pressure, up to 9–10 newtons (300 lb/sq. in) in some calculations. (This does vary hugely according to age and circumstance.[6]) Jaw shape is one rule-of-thumb response to the most frequently asked question about crocodilians: what is the difference between alligators and crocodiles?

A 19th-century impression of the semi-mythical 'trochilus' bird, picking up morsels.

Alligators have broad, shovel-shaped snouts completely covering the teeth; crocodiles have V-shaped snouts revealing the bottom teeth. (Since the Alligatoridae include the highly variable caimans, however, this rule doesn't always hold; one has to look also for the presence of lingual salt glands and DPRS, both of which alligators lack, and for subtler DNA variations bespeaking their divergent lineages.) Crocodilian jaws are, oddly, easily held closed, a trait exploited by crocodile entertainers around the world. For centuries it was thought, following Herodotus, that the crocodilian had no tongue at all. It does, but it is anchored along its length to the floor of the mouth, and plays no part in holding or manoeuvring a meal.

comme lui
lavez-vous
les dents

So, as the jaws clamp, the neck and back surge from the water, powerfully muscled beneath the signature armour of hardened scales or scutes – hence the etymology of the name 'crocodile' itself, from the Greek *kroko* and *deilos*, literally 'pebble-worm'. The most prominent scutes develop bony deposits called osteo-derms, which are not mere horn or bone but well-supplied with blood, enabling rapid heat transference during basking. Story after story relates how unwary travellers or river dwellers have stood on a crocodile's dark back, mistaking it for a submerged log, though in truth you would have to be half blind not to see the regular ridging – as this Ghanaian proverb recognizes: *Ko leggal booyii ley ndiyam, laatataako noora* (even if a log stays for ages in the water, it never becomes a crocodile). Those hard dorsal osteoderms, unlike the surprisingly supple skin of sides and belly, are an important resource for palaeontologists exhuming crocodilian fossils.

Beneath that forbidding back, the ribcage encloses unique breathing, blood distribution and digestive systems. Above water, the lungs are operated by a kind of syringe-plunger effect, compressed and released by abdominal muscles and a primitive diaphragm. The heart, like a mammal's, is four-chambered, but has the feature (present in the human foetus but unique among reptiles) of a valve between the two ventricles. This is the foramen of Panizza, through which blood can be circulated directly round the body when submerged. Blood cells' high oxygen retention means a crocodile can remain submerged for up to two hours. However, the exact timing and operation of unoxygenated and oxygenated blood flow in crocodile life remain subject to argu-ment.[7] The blood also contains, as Australian researcher Adam Britton, together with Gill Diamond of the New Jersey Medical School, discovered in 2002, powerfully antibiotic peptides sub-sequently called crocodillin: hence, apparently, crocodiles' injuries, even in unhygienic waters, heal extremely quickly. The precise qualities of this extraordinary capacity vary subtly from species to species, and indeed distinguish them.[8] A crocodillin-based nostrum

The back of a Nile crocodile, armoured with osteoderms.

named 'The Antidote' was quickly marketed, claiming miraculous efficacy against everything from HIV to cancer; in fact, full clinical trials have yet to be conducted.

Heart and blood together enhance crocodilians' remarkable thermo-regulation mechanisms – another strong factor in surviving past climatic changes. Blood flow to the extremities can be altered and heart rate slowed; but crocodilians are basically poikilothermic – that is, dependent on the environment for heat regulation. So their methods are behavioural more than internal: judicious basking or submerging, depending on ambient temperatures, keeps the body close to around 33°C (91°F). The American and Chinese alligators survive near-freezing temperatures by digging out deep burrows; Florida's characteristic 'gator holes' often contain water, which is less subject to temperature variation than air. Most crocodilians create burrows or occupy caves to escape intense heat or survive drought. Some shy, poaching-threatened crocodiles in Madagascar survive almost entirely confined to deep caves, feeding minimally on blindworms, eels, bats and rodents and weathering the cold by adjusting their metabolisms.

As prey, you are probably least interested in what happens to you after you're swallowed, but you'll pass through a three-chambered stomach, divided into the smooth-walled frontal cardiac region; the gizzard-like, rough-walled fundus; and the rear, enzyme-rich pyloric section. You'll join fragments of insects, fish, frogs, crabs, smaller reptiles including, quite possibly, other crocs, hooves of a buffalo or wallaby nails. There may even be a variety of vegetable matter (caimans eat philodendron fruit; alligators like kumquats;[9] and most will consume some digestion-enhancing greens). The environment down there is exceptionally acid (pH <2), though it will take some time to digest your bones, chitin and hair. Unlucky you. More than half of a crocodile population at any time will usually be empty-stomached; Nile crocodiles probably eat no more than 50 times a year. Moreover, an individual can survive for up to two years with minimal food, subsiding into a slumberous state of aestivation and drawing on fat reserves stored around the body, mostly abdominal.

No aspect of crocodilian digestion has attracted more interest than the presence of stones in the stomach, or gastroliths. In the earliest known reference, in 1688, one Dr D. Stubbs proposed their purpose was to grind up food.[10] More than 200 years later, Yale Peabody Museum researchers, utilizing a dead mouse injected with radio-opaque material, confirmed that the gastroliths seemed responsible for crushing up the little corpse. In 1962 Hugh Cott in *New Scientist*, in one of the first thorough studies of crocodilian behaviour, theorized that they acted as ballast. Both are possible. In people's spiritual systems everywhere, gastroliths acquired mystical significance. Among the Thonga of southern Mozam - bique, for example, they were important in divination; if a chief were treated with suitable drugs, he could swallow a gastrolith, whence it would warn him of his death.[11]

The crocodile's short legs seem faintly comical, necessitating the characteristic waddling walk; but they can propel the crocodile into frightening mobility. Cott first distinguished three modes of crocodilian locomotion: the crawling 'belly walk'; the 'high walk', cumbersome but raising the body completely off the ground; and the 'gallop', sustainable over short distances and up to 13 mph (20 km/h). Remarkably, it wasn't until 1974 that George Zug could claim to have adequately filmed and quantified the details of these gaits.[12] Though the crocodile is capable of moving considerable distances over land if necessary, its favoured mode of movement is swimming, the great tail sinuously driv - ing the body forward with some guidance from the clawed and partially webbed back feet.

Even such heavy tails are not used for batting prey off their feet.

To end, then, with the massively muscled tail. It is not, as legend has it, much used to sweep prey off its feet, but is the main propulsion unit in the launch out of the water. Though it certainly cannot take its owner over the side of a boat, as the pulp-horror film *Crocodile* (2000) portrays, it can propel the creature vertically until almost all the abdomen emerges: salt-water crocodiles pluck flying foxes from overhanging branches in Polynesia. Even birds can be taken this way – including the dead chickens used by crocodile-park entertainers to provoke the leap for public titillation.

Hunting efficiency, superb camouflage and physical resilience are of little avail if an organism cannot reproduce successfully. Survival rates of crocodile hatchlings, vulnerable to monitors, mongooses, monkeys, marabou storks and more (including other crocodiles), are surprisingly low – often less than 10 per cent, even without human impacts. Reproductive behaviour amongst crocodilians is surprisingly complex and nuanced. Male dominance governs at least some sexual access: fights between rivals are largely ritualistic, but can result in serious if not fatal injuries. Amongst more subtle olfactory and tactile signals, males will woo females by blowing bubbles through the nostrils or mouth, or slap their jaws on the water's surface until a mutual lifting and rubbing of heads leads to copulation.[13] This occurs rather awkwardly under water, the male atop the female and wrapping his tail under hers to effect penetration of her cloacal slit. Through their reproductive lives – roughly from the age of twelve years onwards, though size may be more important – some crocodilians seem to remain monogamously paired as long as practicable.

The female, some five months after fertilization, lays a clutch of anything from sixteen to 80 eggs, in a site carefully chosen and retained throughout the female's life. Buried in sand at a depth of 30–38 cm (12–15 in) – or, in the case of caimans and alligators, beneath mounds of rotting vegetation – the eggs incubate for about 90 days, the mother keeping guard, without eating, in the vicinity. Sometimes the dominant male patrols nearby and fends off sub-ordinates. Much research has been devoted to the peculiar effect of temperature on the sex of the offspring. Incubate a nest of alligator eggs at below 32°C (90°F), and predominantly females will develop; at just a degree or two higher, males. Ambient temperatures have substantial effects, and as climate change raises temperatures, researchers worry that nests will produce only a single sex. Some speculate, however, that females will test out nest sites with a view to choosing sex ratios, and deliberately bury eggs at different levels – and clearly, severe climatic changes in past ages have not prevented effective breeding.

Rare photograph of a Brazilian giant otter eating a caiman.

After a variable incubation period, typically eight to twelve weeks, the babies begin to chirrup. The mother (sometimes the father, too) helps free them, and often carries them with astonishing delicacy in her jaws to the water's edge. There they are largely left to defend themselves, though the parents linger for a 'crèche period' of up to twelve weeks. On average, a mere 5 to 10 per cent of the eggs laid result in hatchlings that grow to the age of two. Even as adults, crocodilians are not invulnerable. Jaguars and giant otters prey on South American caimans; leopards and lions, African crocodiles. The hardiest crocodilians can survive for decades; the oldest recorded may be 'Čabulitis', an American alligator who died in Riga Zoo, Latvia, in 2007, aged over 72.

Overall, though, and vulnerabilities notwithstanding, this remarkable physiology has permitted the crocodilian lineage to persist in recognizable forms for at least 200 million years. So let's reach back towards that beginning.

The history of crocodilian evolution is, inevitably, also the history of palaeontology, and of the developing techniques and criteria of phylogeny and taxonomy. Aristotle painstakingly observed animal physiology, and understandably grouped crocodiles with lizards and other 'oviparous quadrupeds'. In his pioneering taxonomic system of 1758, Linnaeus lumped almost all crocodilians under one composite species, *Lacerta crocodilus*. A decade later, J. N. Laurenti proposed four species in the genus *Crocodylus* (a spelling more recently revived), but these were based on vague and derivative drawings executed by one Albertus Seba in 1734. In 1933 Leonhard Stejneger reacted testily to a proposed reintroduction of Laurenti's dodgy scheme; it 'would be nothing less than catastrophic', he cried.[14]

Such finicky disagreement over *existing* crocodilians was only given more scope when the discovery of crocodilian fossils necessitated study of the evolutionary lineages as well. As early as 1834 Georges Cuvier, followed in 1875 by Darwin's friend Thomas Huxley, began to recognize differences between fossil and living crocodilians. Skulls being the most persistent remains, attention focused on the disposition of the internal nares or inner nasal passages, secondarily on the shape of vertebrae. But fossil collecting remained a hit-and-miss, even amateur, affair

Crocodilian fossil, St Augustine Alligator Farm, Florida.

until well into the twentieth century, as evidenced by a rather sweet entry in the *Irish Naturalist* of October 1904, in which one Wm. Christy of Belfast humbly celebrates being 'fortunate' to find a solitary, 'slightly abraded' crocodile scute 'while geologizing' in the Greensand of Colin Glen. Even after the advent of an increasingly professionalized palaeontology, the paucity of fossil material left enormous gaps in knowledge. After the end of the Triassic, for example, 'there is a gap of some millions of years in the crocodilian fossil record'.[15] Hence every meagre find could spawn a new theory of evolutionary lines. In 1927, for example, Robert Broom in South Africa challenged the orthodoxy on the strength of a crocodilian fossil dubbed *Sphenosuchus*.[16]

A new theory of biogeographic links between South America and Indo-Pakistan is based on crocodilian remains found in Pakistan; and more than 100 million years of fossil records from Thailand's Khorat Plateau abruptly threw new light on the whole geologic history of Southeast Asia.[17] The variety of types and spread of discoveries through every continent – even the Arctic – is extraordinary.

New scientific technologies also generate new debates. Morphological analyses were standard from Aristotle to Darwin: Huxley's division of ancient crocodilians into three groups – the Parasuchia, Mesosuchia and Eusuchia – has persisted on morphological grounds to the present. This method has been amplified, though not replaced, by molecular, protein-based or biochemical analyses, which started as early as 1897. But 'preliminary results from both methodologies are interestingly still contradictory'.[18] Herbert Dessauer, who worked on molecular analysis of alligator evolution for decades, humorously revealed the more mundane aspects of this increasingly specialized research: 'One learned to handle alligators, collect their body fluids and maintain them in captivity. Often the day would begin with an alligator roundup, following the escape of our specimens from their cadaver tank homes.' In the end, Dessauer adds, 'Relationships within the Crocodylia, while perhaps better understood than ever, are far from incontrovertible.'[19]

Meanwhile, DNA analyses and dating via mitochondrial RNA (Ribonucleic Acid) genome sequencing has taken centre stage. Genetic sequencing was first completed for the American alli-gator (*A. mississippiensis*), leading researchers Axel Janke and Ulfur Arnason of the University of Lund to conclude in 1997 that a divergence between birds and crocodilian ancestries occurred around 254 million years ago.[20] Counter-intuitively, crocodil-ians seem to be more closely related to birds than to lizards or monitors. Amongst numerous finds, fossilized eggshells excavated from Eocene sands near Parachute, Colorado in 1958 – which had to wait until 1985 and the invention of polarizing light microscopy, scanning electron microscopy and x-ray fluorescence for confirmation that they were crocodilian at all – now seem to bolster this.[21] The comparative data, however, is still scanty.

At least we can say that, between the two great extinction events of 250 and 65 MYA, crocodilians shared the planet with dinosaurs of all shapes and sizes, and themselves proliferated in numerous lineages of shorter or longer duration. Very roughly, protosuchians – primitive crocodilians – appear almost world - wide amongst Triassic-period archosaurs. Mesosuchians appear around 190 MYA, beginning to evolve into eusuchians – modern crocodilians with ball-and-socket vertebrae and distinctive skull apertures – in the early Cretaceous, 140 MYA.[22] At the level of detail, classifications have flowered and died, subspecies named and controversially renamed: dryosaurids and pristichampsines, Hylaeochampsa and Boralosuchus, Leidyosuchus and Barchychampsa, and many more.[23] While crocodilians have become almost by definition aquatic, recent fossils suggest that some of the earliest were terrestrial. In 2009 Joseph Sertich, in the Rukwa Rift Basin of Tanzania, excavated the complete skeleton of a creature dubbed *Pakasuchus* (from the kiSwahili *paka* meaning 'cat' and the Greek *suchus*, for crocodile). *Pakasuchus* was built like a crocodile but had molar teeth like a mammal's, forward-facing nostrils, and limbs that suggest a land-based lifestyle. In northwest Africa, Paul Sereno has documented a raft of species that ranged over what was then Gondwana, before the continents began splitting up around 200 MYA. So-called BoarCroc (*Kaprosuchus saharicus*) was a 6.1-m (20-ft) carnivore with an armoured snout and warthog-like tushes; RatCroc (*Ararispesuchus rattoides*) was barely

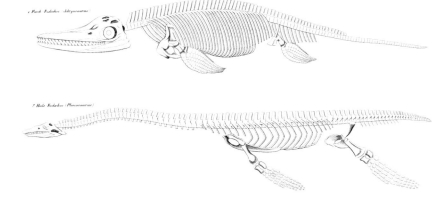

1 m (3 ft) long, a buck-toothed plant- and grub-eater; and Pancake-Croc (*Laganosuchus thaumastos*), whose whole flat head measured 1 m (3 ft) long, waited on unwary fish with elongated jaws.

Sereno became an instant celebrity when *National Geographic* publicized his discovery of 'SuperCroc'. In fact, fossils of this giant, *Sarcosuchus imperator*, had been found in the Ténéré Desert in Niger as early as 1964, but were under-studied until Sereno found more complete remains in the Sahara. Broad-snouted, unlike its narrow-jawed, fish-eating contemporaries, with 40-odd massive triangular teeth, its skull alone measured nearly 2 m (6 ft) – the documentary footage of Sereno lying down *inside* the exposed jawline of this huge creature is unforgettable. Taking modern crocodilian proportions as a guide, Sereno could extrapolate a total length for SuperCroc of nearly 12.2 m (40 ft) and a weight of some 8 tons (17,500 lb). That this appears as much dinosaur as crocodile is strengthened by Sereno's surmise that SuperCroc in fact existed on a parallel lineage to that which eventuated in modern crocodilians. Fortunately for us, SuperCroc died out some 80 MYA.[24]

This last irrefutable fact notwithstanding, creationist Peter Booker thinks *Sarcosuchus* makes a fine candidate for Leviathan, as described in Job 41:

> His scales are his pride, shut up together as with a close seal
> One is so near to another, that no air can come between
>   them . . .
> He esteemeth iron as straw, and brass as rotten wood;
> The arrow cannot make him flee; slingstones are turned
>   with him into stubble . . .
> His snorting throws out flashes of light; his eyes are like
>   the rays of dawn.
> Firebrands stream from his mouth; sparks of fire shoot
>   out;
> Smoke pours from his nostrils as from a boiling pot over
>   a fire of reeds.
> His breath sets coals ablaze, and flames dart from his
>   mouth.

Booker undermines himself by quoting Job's own statement that Leviathan was sea-going, which *Sarcosuchus* was not; and relies heavily on some inconsequential parallels of phrasing between Job and Sereno's *National Geographic* article. When Booker speculates that *Sarcosuchus* used its unusually large nasal cavity to generate fire, we know we are in the realm of overstrained fantasy – and the notion that Leviathan itself might be fantasy, along similar lines to European and Chinese 'crocodyliform' dragons, does not occur to him.[25]

That some crocodilians *were* – and are – sea-going is true enough. A whole putative family of extinct crocodilians is termed 'thalassosuchians' (from the Greek *thalassa*, meaning 'ocean'). Debate continues about how crocodilians spread across the

planet after the super-continent of Gondwana disintegrated. Were they able to swim, or raft; were there convenient land bridges; did they evolve differentially from a single source, or convergently in different places, or both? Much attention has focused on the subfamily now known as *gavialis*, the gharials or gavials, narrow-snouted species represented today only by the Indian gharial (*Gavialis gangeticus*) and (possibly) the Indonesian false gharial (*Tomistoma schlegelii*). Both are freshwater fish-eaters unlikely to have dispersed across oceans. Ambiguously, they possess a keratinized oral cavity, a feature thought to limit osmotic loss of body fluids in saline waters, theoretically making oceanic travel possible; but they lack the large, salt-excreting glands found on the tongues of other sea-going species, such as the saltwater crocodile (*Crocodylus porosus*). Yet gavialoid remains have been found on almost every continent, dating from the Late Creta-ceous through the Palaeocene, and almost all in shallow marine deposits. Tentatively, then, crocodilian expert Christopher Brochu, basing his theory on a new Puerto Rican fossil found *c.* 2005, proposes a whole clade of gavialoid oceanic travellers which might have crossed the (then narrower) Atlantic from Africa – or from Asia. Moreover, the most recent mitochondrial genome sequencing of African and American crocodiles suggests so recent a parting of genetic ways that their ancestors could only have migrated by swimming the Atlantic.[26]

Such oceanic migrations apart, the splitting of the continents increasingly isolated crocodilian populations, although hybridiz-ation between adjacent species then (and even now) complicates

Plesiosaurus gavial.

A giant rock engraving on Libya's Messak plateau, 17 m long and 10,000 years old, testifies to a wetter era.

clear taxonomic definitions. Simultaneously, a cooling global climate drove crocodilians entirely out of the northern regions into the tropical zones where they are to be found today. By the end of the Miocene (5 MYA), European alligators and gavials were all but extinct. In the tropics, numerous now-vanished species, such as giant eusuchians in South America, survived into the Late Tertiary. Out of all the varied strains of 180 million years of evolutionary proliferation, the family Crocodylidae today contains 23 recognized species from three major subfamilies, the *Crocodylidae*, the *Gavialidae* and the *Alligatoridae*, the divergence between which probably occurred within the last 50 million years. It is evidence of the global distribution of ancient crocodilians, and of their persistence in a wide range of habitats and climates, that these families do not entirely correlate with regions or continent. But by continent, roughly, starting in Africa and moving eastwards round the globe, we will now proceed. To Africa – just because it's my home, but also fantastically rich in relevant lore – I shall devote the, well, crocodile's share.

2 North and West Africa

Africa seems preternaturally rich in crocodile lore, both fearful and reverential, from the world's most ancient folktales to modern syncretic art. The shifting varieties of this lore over four millennia will be this chapter's primary theme, as we glean examples from the continent's two major northern river systems: the Nile and the Niger.

Two species of African crocodile have all but escaped the outside world's notice: the slender-snouted crocodile (formerly *Crocodylus*, now *Mecistops cataphractus*) and the West African dwarf or broad-snouted crocodile (*Osteolaemus tetraspis*). Both range across western Africa from northern Angola to Mauretania; both remain poorly known, and are listed as vulnerable by the IUCN (International Union for Conservation of Nature). Both are subject to some taxonomic dispute. The slender-snouted crocodile (its Latin name is derived from the Greek *kataphraktos*, 'clad in armour') is mostly fish-eating and relatively small – at most 3.7 m (12 ft) – despite its alternative forbidding name of 'Panzer crocodile'. Its narrow snout gave rise to one of its French names, 'faux-gharial'. Its stronghold is in Gabon, particularly in lakes but also in brackish coastal waters, even on the offshore Bioko Island. Habitat destruction and local skin trade has reduced its numbers to only some 50,000.[1]

The dwarf crocodile never exceeds 2 m (6 ft), though it is heavily armoured for its size: hence both its Latin names,

Osteolaemus ('bony throat') and *tetraspis* ('four shields'), referring to bony scales on the neck. Two subspecies are currently recognized, *O. t. tetraspis* and *O. t. osborni* or Osborn's crocodile, which is confined to the Democratic Republic of Congo. Nocturnal, favouring sluggish rainforest waters and mostly fish- and crustacean-eating, this species is regarded as less at risk from the skin trade than from local meat consumption. Monitoring and knowledge of the species remains extremely patchy; between 25,000 and 100,000 individuals exist.

So, as throughout history, these two minor species must remain overshadowed by the best-known behemoth of them all. The Nile crocodile (*C. niloticus*) inhabits most of Africa, excepting the desert regions. Some biological variability over this huge range has prompted suggestions for various subspecies, including West African, East African or Kenyan, South African and Malagasy varieties, but none are currently officially recognized. Recent research by Evon Hekkala of Fordham University uses DNA samples

African dwarf or broad-snouted crocodile.

sequenced from 123 living individuals and 57 museum specimens (including 2,000-year-old Egyptian mummies) to suggest two species. *C. niloticus* now appears more closely related to the four New World crocodiles than to the 'new' one, dubbed *C. suchus*.[2] Externally, however, they are indistinguishable, and for present purposes we'll regard them as one.

Adaptable to a wide range of diets and habitats, Nile crocodiles naturally grow to around 4.9 m (16 ft), but very occasionally up to 6.1 m (20 ft). The largest on record, shot by the Duke of Mecklenburg in Tanzania in 1905, allegedly stretched over 6.4 m (21 ft) and weighed some 2,300 lb (1043 kg) – but the official record is a 1953 Ugandan specimen measuring 5.8 m (19 ft) with a girth of 2.24 m (7 ft). In harsher, dry environments such as Mali's Sahel region, in contrast, they have adaptively dwarfed down. Hence overall, despite some three million killed for the skin trade between 1950 and 1980 alone,[3] possibly 500,000 remain in the wild, alongside successful captive farming and breeding in many places. Nile crocodiles probably kill two to three hundred people in Africa every year, but there is no monitoring system, and many must go unreported. The species has nevertheless come close to being eliminated from some regions, especially in West and central Africa. At the edges of its range, it was hunted to extinction from the Seychelles and Comoro Islands in the 1800s, and much more recently from Israel. It disappeared from the Nile delta as early as 1700, and by 1972 from all of Egypt, though some Nile crocodiles have returned since the Aswan Dam was built.

The Nile River is a good place to start our African survey. Drawing on the beliefs of their animistic African precursors, the ancient Egyptians developed one of the world's most complex, long-lived, artistically sophisticated and architecturally unique civilizations and spiritual systems. As early as the Old Kingdom (*c.* 2686–2181 BCE), over 200 gods and goddesses had acquired distinctive names and characteristics. Simplistically, these figures could be regarded as embodying particular natural forces to be supplicated, revered or symbolically combated, but they could also be attached to particular places and associated cults, with quite different qualities from one locale or time to another. Still more confusingly, they could be melded to form syncretic embodiments of natural powers and processes from which human supplicants would try to gain or protect themselves. Moreover, through the millennia of the Middle and New Kingdoms (*c.* 2055–1650 BCE and 1550–1069 BCE respectively), and into the late and Graeco-Roman periods (up to *c.* 400 CE), political power struggles created successive dynasties, successively split and reunited Egypt and successively warded off, conquered and succumbed to foreign powers. Hence the meanings attached to the swarming cultic figures changed and accreted in a multiplicity of contradictory ways. Part resource, part terrifying enemy, the crocodile thus unsurprisingly comes to play antithetical roles in the Egyptian pantheon.

The rhythms and denizens of the Nile, the primary life-source for all Egyptians, inevitably provided elements for ancient Egyptian thought patterns and art. One of the earliest known creation myths features the motherly Neith, whose sexual union with Khnum created forces of both chaos and order, initiating the Nile's annual flood, inventing childbirth and giving form to the life-affirming sun god. In some versions, she utters seven magical words which form the known world – a mythic expression of the birth of language. Early representations of animals and objects developed into hieroglyphic script capable of bearing both complex symbolic meanings and representing linguistic sounds. Hence the crocodile, among other such representations, features naturalistically on the 'Metternich stela', a collection of incantations largely set in marshlands; but as a determinative the crocodile signified the power of kingly or pharaonic authority, and even, in the cases of the eight rulers of the thirteenth dynasty, was a component of their birth name, Sobekhotep. The representation of crocodile skin indicated the syllable 'km', in some instances signifying 'aggression'.

Neith's spit or vomit formed the monster of disorder, Apophis, who along with the crocodile would often be depicted as warring with the sun gods. For Neith also gives birth to Sobek (Sebek, Suchos), the crocodile god. His variable attributes are neatly summarized by Geraldine Pinch:

> Few of Sobek's characteristics were exclusive to him, but together they formed a unique divine profile: he shared his crocodile form with other gods such as Seth and Khenty-khet; like Seth, he could be regarded as the strongest of the gods; like Min, he was the most virile of the gods, able to satisfy any number of goddesses; like Hapy, the spirit of the inundation (annual Nile flood), he was praised for 'greening' the desert; he was a local god to people in the Fayum area who lived around a lake full of crocodiles; he was the protector of those who worked on or near water, such as fishermen, bird-catchers and washermen; he was the brutal instrument of fate who snatched people to sudden deaths; he was one of the creatures who embodied the primeval ocean; wearing his 'solar disc' hat, he was the deity who created and sustained the world.[4]

Hence Sobek is sometimes depicted being speared or crushed underfoot by Horus, son of Osiris, as on a stela from the Ptolemaic period (*c.* 400 BCE). Spells on the stela indicate that, with the right incantations, liquid poured over the stone would be charged with equivalent power and consumed by the devotee for protection

or medicinal cure. Elsewhere, contradictorily, Sobek is implicated positively both in the birth of Horus, and in retrieving the body of the primary god Osiris, drowned or dismembered by his brother Seth.

The crocodile is sometimes depicted in association with another river dweller, the hippopotamus. In one extraordinary relief carving, a beautifully observed crocodile seems about to snap at the head of a baby hippo just emerging from its mother's rear – a natural event, to be sure, but also possibly an allusion to the birth of a solar form of Osiris. In others, a hippo goddess-figure, usually known as Taweret, appears to carry a crocodile vertically on her back, as on the ceiling painting of the tomb of Seti I at Thebes, Valley of the Kings. Nearby, another crocodile seems attached to, or is being fed by, the hand of a humanoid figure. The scene is said to represent the death of the king, and is usually interpreted as a representation of various constellations. In other representations, Taweret appears as a composite of hippo body and head, with humanoid breasts of fecundity, the claws of a lion and the tail of a crocodile, thus blending all the fruitful and fearful qualities of the transition into death and rebirth.

Most often, Sobek appears united with the sun god Ra: in a seven-ton calcite statue now in the Luxor Museum, this composite god features both his crocodile head and Ra's solar-disc headdress, embraces in avuncular fashion a youthful-looking pharaoh, Amenhotep III (c. 1391–1353 BCE), and hands him the mystic *ankh*, symbol of life itself. His animal side represents natural power, longevity, cunning; his human body his accessibility and succour. Something of the contradictoriness is caught in a hymn from a papyrus roll in the 'Ramesseum library':

Hail to you, who arose from the primeval waters,
lord of the lowlands, ruler of the desert edge,

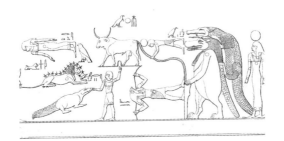

A 19th-century German drawing of the Seti tomb ceiling, Nile Valley. The hippo-related goddess Taweret presides over funerary rites, attended by crocodiles.

who crosses backwaters;
mighty god, whose seizing cannot be seen,
who lives on plunder,
who goes upstream by his [own] perfection,
who goes downstream, after hunting a multitude . . .[5]

Nowhere was the crocodile more prominent in real and mythic life than in the Fayum, the marshland west of the Nile where Sobek was regarded as a protector and imposer of order. While elsewhere crocodile-hunting was a sport, here killing them was taboo. Diodorus Siculus (90–30 BCE) traced the reverence for crocodiles to a story about how King Menes is chased into the Fayum's Lake Moeris by his own dogs, but is saved by a crocodile in return for help against a water demon. Hence, it was said, Menes founded the city of Arsinoë, named by the Greeks Krokodilopolis, where crocodiles were kept in temple pools and fed. Perhaps the best known of all Sobek images is the relief carving at the entrance of the temple of Kom-Ombo, on the southern Nile.

Kom-Ombo is the primary site for the most astonishing manifestation of crocodile worship: mummies. The Egyptians mummified everything – cats and dogs, rams and shrews, fish and hawks, even beetles and haunches of beef. At various sites crocodiles were found mummified in their hundreds; one spectacular specimen, now in the Egyptian Museum, measured over 5.5 m (17 ft) and had baby crocodile mummies cradled in its mouth; someone had observed their natural behaviour closely. It was also thought that, because crocodiles seemed uncannily to predict the height of impending floodwaters and to lay their eggs accordingly, they could foretell the future; they were therefore particularly apposite companions for the journey into the afterlife. Over weeks of preparation – disembowelled, dried in natron, wrapped in parchments or linen and buried with due ceremony – crocodiles were given their place in the ranks of the spiritual dead.[6]

There is yet another fascinating layer. The story goes that in the 1890s, a workman digging for human mummies unearthed a dried-out crocodile and casually tossed it aside; it split open on impact, revealing an interior stuffed with papyri. It turned out that dozens of these crocodiles were stuffed or wrapped with discarded documents mostly dating from the Graeco-Roman period (332 BCE–440 CE) and written in hieroglyphic, demotic, Coptic, Greek and even Latin. They include commercial transactions, letters, bills, lists, marriage contracts and even fragments of literature: plays by Euripides and Sophocles and episodes from Plato and Homer. Tens of thousands of these fragments, many excavated by Grenfell and Hunt at Tebtunis in the southern Fayum in 1895–6, have found their way to repositories in Berlin, London, Lecce and Copenhagen; 45,000 are housed in the USA alone. Most languish undeciphered, though a consortium of universities and museums dubbed (after another Egyptian god) APIS, or Advanced Papyrological Information Symposium, is making available on the Internet more of these extraordinary treasures, unexpectedly rescued from the bellies of crocodiles two millennia old.[7]

Papyri also hold some of the oldest, originally oral, myths of Egyptian life. Part legendary and magical, part pharaonic history,

a number contain crocodile references and characters – most often forbiddingly punitive. One is conventionally entitled 'King Khufui and the Magicians', first translated into English in a synopsis by the great Egyptologist Flinders Petrie in 1895. The papyrus consists of stories apparently related to King Cheops by his sons one day when he was feeling depressed. One of the stories tells of how a certain King Nabka, while visiting his chief lector Ubau-anir at the temple of Ptah, becomes aware that the lector's wife has been sneaking off to a 'kiosque' or pavilion on the 'lake of Ubau-anir' for some hanky-panky with a handsome vassal. The miscreants are betrayed by the kiosque's major-domo:

> When the chief lector, Ubau-anir, knew these things that had happened in his kiosque, he said to the major-domo 'Bring me my ebony casket adorned with electrum that contains my book of magic.' When the major-domo had brought it, he modelled a crocodile in wax, seven inches long, he recited over it that which he recited from his book

of magic; he said to it: 'When that vassal comes to bathe in my lake, then drag him to the bottom of the water.'

Accordingly, when the vassal swims, the major-domo throws the wax crocodile in after him; it becomes real, and drags the vassal down. But this is not the end; after seven days, Ubau-anir presents himself to King Nabka and invites him to witness a marvel at the lakeside:

> Ubau-anir said to the crocodile, 'Bring the vassal out of the water.' The crocodile came forth and brought the vassal out of the water. The first lector, Ubau-anir, said, 'Let him stop,' and he conjured him, he caused him to stop in front of the king. Then his Majesty, the King of Upper and Lower Egypt, Nabka, true of voice, said, 'I pray you! this crocodile is terrifying.' Ubau-anir stooped, he seized the crocodile, and it became in his hands only a crocodile of wax.

When Nabka learns of the original misdemeanour, however, he instructs the crocodile, 'Take that which is thine'; the crocodile plunges back to the bottom of the lake, 'and it is not known further what became of the vassal and of it'.[8]

The linkage between crocodiles as a common threat and the ritualized practices of divinely sanctioned punishment emerges also in a story, usually titled 'The Doomed Prince', perhaps dating from the twentieth dynasty, but thought by some to be 'the world's oldest fairy tale'.[9] Here, an unnamed king or prince, some Hathors ('fairy godmothers') predict, will die by giant, serpent, crocodile or dog. Attempts to avoid this destiny are inevitably futile. The crocodile enters the story at a late stage, proclaiming: 'Lo, I am thy destiny that pursues thee.'[10] That fate was in many parts of Egypt depicted as the weighing of the heart – and one's deeds – in the judicial scales of ibis-headed Thoth. The crocodilian Sobek often oversaw the process.

The glory and longevity of ancient Egypt has drawn writers and travellers to North Africa, its attractions eclipsing the even longer stretch of the Nile south of Elephantine Island. River dwellers from present-day Sudan, Ethiopia and northern Kenya have had an equally long relationship with the crocodile, but it is less well documented. In Ethiopia, for example, the ravenous jaws of the crocodile are figured in the colourful illuminated manuscripts and church decorations of the longest-living Christian sect in the world. One, the 'Icon of the Resurrection' is an early sixteenth-century depiction, heavily influenced by Nicolò Brancaleon and painted in tempera on gesso-covered wooden boards; it shows Christ raising Adam from amongst the souls of purgatory, while the Devil in hell swallows down the condemned with crocodilian jaws.[11] In these widely divergent cultures, then, the crocodile commonly symbolizes the unpredictable, implacable judicial power of the gods themselves – an iconography which surely originates even further back in time, among black African animist worldviews. Glimpses of that world – earthy, physical and infinitely complex – can still be found throughout West Africa, in particular along the banks of the Niger River.

Like the Nile, the Niger debouches into the sea in a great delta; it traverses a region long torn by conflict as well as enriched by great blendings of culture: African, Muslim, European, Indian. From its headwaters among the small countries on Africa's western coast to its Nigerian delta, people have revered the crocodile for millennia. In the Ivory Coast, that acerbic observer and novelist V. S. Naipaul, in a famous essay entitled 'The Crocodiles of Yamoussoukro' (1984), made a connection to Egypt. He had visited a pool at the Ivorian president's extravagant palace at

In Mali, carvings of crocodiles outside homes symbolize hospitality.

Yamoussoukro, where crocodiles were fed black chickens and had on occasion eaten a person, not necessarily accidentally. Behind the modern setting in its artificial, iron-railed lake, guarded by men with firearms, Naipaul discerns the traces of far older, elusive symbolisms, 'a remnant of ancient Egyptian earth-worship, coming down and across to black Africa across the Sudan'.[12] It was almost certainly the other way round, new Egyptian power structures extrapolating and attenuating the original black African animist systems.

There was surely also a simpler, common, visceral symbolism generated by the crocodile itself. Something of the frisson of primordial fear energizes Naipaul's own vivid description of the reptiles:

A Dogon door, Mali.

absolutely still, eyes bright and apparently unseeing, jaws open, the lower jaw of each crocodile showing only as a great hollow, oddly simple in shape, oddly clean and

dry-looking, yellow-pink and pale. Flies moved in and out of those open jaws.[13]

This same primordial horror was caught by Senegal's president-poet Léopold Senghor in his poem 'L'Homme et la bête' (Man and the Beast): 'But the Beast is without form in the fecund mud, breeding mosquito and tsetse, / . . . crocodiles [caimans] with mouths of cactus.'[14]

Yamoussoukro is not the only place where crocodiles are ritually succoured. At its northernmost point, the Niger curves through Mali, where crocodiles have gained the status of protectors, even as symbols of hospitality. Mali's Dogon, the 'People of the Cliffs', conceive of a three-god universe: the Janus-faced sky god Ama; the earth god Lewe; and a water god, Nomo. Nomo is particularly capricious, arbitrarily drowning people in rivers or floods. Frogs and crocodiles are thus her amphibious familiars, to be ritually appeased. Crocodiles which aestivate for weeks or months in damp cliff recesses during dry periods emerge into a sacred pool at the Dogon village of Amani, where a priest serves up chickens or a goat at ritual (and touristic) moments. (Another such sacred pool is at Bazoulé in Burkina Faso.) Wooden Dogon doors are typically decorated with crocodile carvings, and from the characteristic red-mud walls of Malian buildings jut blue-white wooden carvings of crocodiles. Sometimes hybridized with or indistinguishable from lizards, relief sculptures and wall paintings celebrate the crocodile, often schematized into the triangular lozenge pattern of crocodile skin.

The crocodile's association with kingly power manifested particularly in Benin, flourishing from the twelfth century onwards: the spiritual leader or oba's palace was adorned with metal plaques, among them the crocodile, emphasizing the oba's close connection with the life-giving water of the river. More everyday associations also produced beautiful artefacts. A cylindrical brass box from Akan, in Ghana, is embossed with two crocodiles tail-to-nose, illustrating the proverb *'funtum frafu denkyem frafu'* – 'bellies mixed up, crocodiles mixed up' – which is intended to discourage greediness and egoism, since no matter which crocodile eats the food it still goes to the same stomach.

People throughout the Niger region still perform placatory rituals and masquerades, especially for rain-making purposes. In these dances, headdresses and masks are of particular importance. Some incorporate the crocodile, made to look like spirits that float on the surface of the water, and occasionally distinctly depict the slender-snouted species. Others appear alongside, or are hybridized with sharks and sawfish. Still others apparently spoof the whole enterprise with comical masks: 'Nevertheless, the hostile, transgressive behaviour they exhibit . . . attempts to beat back hostile spirits and neutralise their power.'[15]

Perhaps the most complex, and most misunderstood, example of African animism is that of *vodun*, the word deriving from the people of that name, eventually to be transported via the slave trade to the Caribbean as 'voodoo' and thence progressively vilified and misrepresented by Christian and scientific Westerners. From Senegal to Burkina Faso, *vodun* as a practice of dealing with the world's unpredictable chthonic forces remains rich, adaptable and earthy. Beneath the major Vodun god figures – Hervioso (or Hevioso), the keeper of justice; Legba, keeper of the crossroads between the physical and spiritual worlds; and Oshun the river goddess, healer and relationship expert – swarm sundry nature spirits, amongst which Adjapta the crocodile is ranked. In the language of the Vodun, the search is to connect with or evoke *bo*, a slippery concept of spiritual power. *Bo*, or *bocio* (from Fon *bo*, empowered, and *cio*, cadaver), can be invoked through ritual objects and chants, often within the precincts of a designated

Copper plaque once attached to a palace wall in Benin, symbolizing royal power.

shrine, for any number of reasons: to attract a client or seduce a lover to induce hatred or immunize oneself against poisoning; to create goodwill, send a sickness, or render a rival impotent. A French traveller in 1863 described one temple of *bo* as

> filled with idols . . . in wood, earth, and ivory, large and small, of human and animal form and even fantasy: serpents,

monkeys, and tigers [sic], dogs with crocodile heads and men with dog heads.

The profusion of objects reflects the virtues of *bo* – as innumerable as 'the manifestations of desire that they have the virtue of realising or enshackling'.[16]

One *bo* sculpture included parts of a crocodile and python: 'Placed one way and the whole of life takes fire', explained an informant; 'placed another way and the rain will fall'. The head of the crocodile is frequently incorporated into *bo* works to prevent water accidents and drowning, or as a revealer of truth, so the term for crocodile (*lo*) also refers to the metaphoric form of wisdom that is imparted in proverbs. Proverbially, the crocodile embodies power or expresses the necessity to fear or avoid

Ghanaian bronze 'box' with cooperative crocodiles.

49

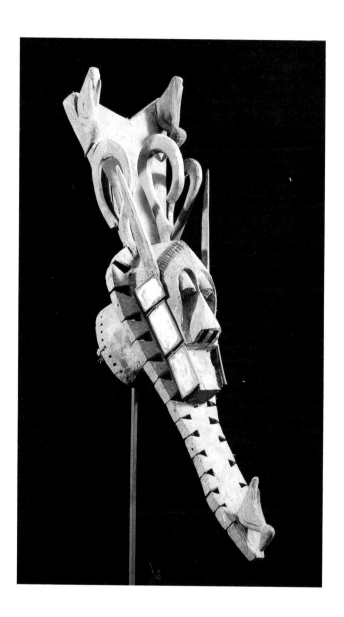

those who are forceful and dominant: 'A fish is a small thing for a crocodile'; 'If a fish wishes to start a quarrel with the crocodile, it is the fish that will die'; 'The scales of the crocodile do not kill the crocodile.' The crocodile's ability to slip out of sight means that if someone is looking for you, you can use crocodile *bo* to avoid him. The strength of the crocodile's jaw can represent silence, so a *bocio* whose mouth is shown bound or blocked, or has a piece of iron inserted in it, signifies that 'this person cannot speak'. Since the animal is so well armoured, crocodile-derived medicine (*muti*) can be deployed to protect oneself from malevolent forces. So, as Suzanne Preston Blier summarizes it, reptilian powers can encompass an enormous range of qualities and processes:

> truth, domination, quarrels, killing, loss, avoidance, drowning, freshness, coolness, fecundity, poison, swallowing, home, calmness, danger, sight, talking, thorns, death, family, history, longevity, accidents, life change, ambiguity, attraction, renewal, swelling, hiding, disappearance and attachment.[17]

Equally variable are Africa's innumerable water divinities, crucial to religious life from Senegal to South Africa. Like crocodiles, they live in the margins, the locus of ambiguity and peril. So, for instance, somewhere in the depths of the Kwa River, in Igbo Nigeria, 'lives Nimm the terrible . . . above all, the object of women's devotion [who] manifests herself sometimes as a huge snake, sometimes as a crocodile'. In the Okigwe area, water goddesses such as Imo, Lolo and Ihuku protect the local community, and 'Before an important person died . . . the deity's crocodile would cry out continually for four days.' They are also implacable forces for moral rectitude whose wishes and regulations must

Composite ritual mask in wood, Niger.

Vodun construction of magical items, including a crocodile jaw.

be obeyed. From Nigeria to Cameroon, special dark places in the forest are thought to be inhabited by the nature spirits (*arem*), some of which might appear in the shape of a crocodile. One secret women's society, in which initiates are graded in terms of arcane knowledge, often builds the crocodile, sometimes hybridized with the python, into their colourful sculptures, paraded on special days.[18]

In a fascinating case of the syncretism of the ancient and the modern, one finds right across Africa various manifestations of the figure of 'Mami Wata' – Mother Water. This is, unmistakably, the legendary European mermaid: long-haired, fair-skinned and bare-breasted, with a silvery fish tail. Scholars argue over precisely how this mermaid got inserted into African religion, but according to Henry John Drewal, the popular image is based on a German chromolithograph of a snake-charmer, *Der Schlan-genbandiger*, introduced shortly before 1900 through the delta regions of Nigeria and thence spreading to other parts of the country and the continent. Joseph Nevadomsky calls this astonishing hybridization 'African arts scholarship's most irrefutably postmodern subject'.[19] From her very first African appearance, apparently, Mami Wata was associated with crocodiles; and crocodiles' roles would vary as radically as her own. In up to 2,000 separate shrine sites in the Ogoni sector of the Niger delta, Mami Wata is evoked as a protective spirit against the depredations of the oil companies and as iconic of Ogoni struggles for independence from central government – and crocodiles are frequently represented as her allies. Contrarily, just a few miles down the coast she appears as a nasty temptress of capitalist

Indian art has influenced this Congo mural, which depicts Mami Wata with devoted crocodile.

greed or sexual predation, and her crocodiles, accordingly, figure as dangerously deceptive threats, would-be attackers clamped in their jaws.

Working along the Benin, Togo and Ghana coasts, Joseph Kossivi Ahiator is an artist who paints murals depicting Mami Wata in a style heavily inflected by Indian art. Indian traders have been visiting West Africa since the fifteenth century, but especially after the First World War local people began integrating Gujeratis (followers of Lakshmi), motifs of Asian divinities, into their works. In one temple mural by Kossivi in Lomé, Togo, painted in 1999, Mami Wata appears behind a multi-armed Shiva figure, overarched by the rainbow serpent. In the foreground appears Ajakpa, the crocodilian 'chauffeur', the mediator between world and underworld, carrying his spiritual weapons: on his head he balances symbols for Heviosso, Vodun diety of thunder and lightning, and Dan the rainbow serpent protruding from a little clay pot; in his mouth he cradles his favourite sustenance, eggs, to all appearances proffering them to the god figure.

Further south, in the Congo, Mami Wata reappears as a hybridized woman-serpent, 'mediating between the world of village traditions and the world of written norms associated with the nation-state and global economy'.[20] One mural in Kinshasa fascinatingly incorporates both Christian and traditional motifs: on the one hand a pastor in white preaching near a graveyard, a devilish monster with '666' on his forehead, and a leopard-patterned serpent of temptation; on the other a traditional *guérisseur* or 'healer', listing his attributes, crouches above a water scene in which a man is being dragged from his dugout canoe by very realistically rendered crocodiles; the latter are presumably protecting Mami Wata who, in the foreground with her customary fair skin, bare breasts, long hair and fish tail, is speaking into a detached, upside-down telephone receiver – a thoroughly modern mode of speaking to the dead who live beneath the river's surface.

But we are drifting here into the geographical space to which the next chapter is devoted: the southern half of this massive and complex continent.

3 Central and Southern Africa

No image of the crocodile is more iconic of its power than that of the plated behemoths waiting patiently for the arrival of the world's greatest terrestrial mammal migration. Every year over 1.5 million wildebeest and zebra head across the plains of the Serengeti in Tanzania to reach fresh grazing grounds: at the jampacked, panicky river crossings, the crocodiles explode from the churning waters and drag the hoofed feasts down. As I began writing this, an international campaign was afoot to prevent the Tanzanian government driving a highway across the northern Serengeti, a 'development' venture which would cut off that magnificent migration route, and probably spell the end for most of those animals – including the crocodiles – and for tourism alike.

Such conflict, between ancient traditions, modern conservation philosophies and the inexorable demands of burgeoning human populations, will be one theme of this chapter as we head roughly southwards from the splayed headwaters of the Congo, down to the Zambezi and the Limpopo (or Crocodile) and across other smaller rivers as far as the Nile crocodile's southernmost habitat, the lagoons of South Africa's St Lucia. A second, intertwined theme continues from the previous chapter: the connections between crocodiles and political power, from pre-colonial to contemporary.

Three instances from the region between the headwaters of the Nile and of the Congo rivers illustrate the contestations. First, Alistair Graham's *Eyelids of Morning* (1973) – the title is from Job's depiction of Leviathan – is perhaps the most vivid book on 'the mingled destinies of crocodiles and men' ever published. Relating 1960s research trips conducted to the still remote Lake Rudolf (Turkana) in Kenya, but incorporating much mythology as it goes, Graham's book is illustrated with Peter Beard's photographs, characteristically ranging from beautiful

Porcelain figure representing 'Africa' with crocodile, *c.* 1770.

to stomach-churning. Graham had little compunction about conducting research by massacring the crocodiles: 'We were to finance it wholly out of what we could get for the skins of the five hundred crocs to be killed for investigation . . . But what [we] really wanted to know was how we thought the crocs on Rudolf fitted in with the growing fishing interest there.' The results he regarded as dubious: 'Our knowledge of crocodiles ultimately was of value only to those far from Lake Rudolf who, feeling overcrowded, needed more resources, more ideas, more space – simply *more*.' He realized:'We stand poised to condemn crocodiles to obliteration, and to captivity and decay in national parks and zoos, or to indifferent dissolution – yet we know scarcely anything about them.' But he had 'no sentimental impulse to "save" crocodiles. If they needed saving it could only be from some disaster common to man as well.' Idiosyncratic, grim and sceptical about current conservationist philosophy, *Eyelids of Morning* remains a unique, dramatically documented paean to the crocodile.[1]

Second: just a little further south and half a century later, a killer croc had reportedly been terrorizing people in Burundi for twenty years. They dubbed him Gustave, claiming he was over 5.9 m (18 ft) long and had eaten 200 people. Determined at first to kill this miscreant, French-born resident Patrice Faye eventually decided rather to catch him and fit him out with a tracking device. The last report was that Gustave had evaded capture, however – as he does at the end of the film *Primeval* (2007), which he inspired.[2]

And third: in a similar clash of practical revulsion and modern conservation policies, in 2005 a marauding crocodile in the Ugandan sector of Lake Victoria was finally snared. Popularly known as Osama and believed to be the spawn of Satan, the crocodile had reputedly eaten 83 people, going so far as to jump into

Baby slender-snouted crocodile.

boats to get them. The villagers were mystified that wildlife officials refused to slaughter the predator, which ended up in a Ugandan crocodile farm, looking depressed at spending 'the rest of his days giving birth to handbags', as the report put it.[3] Yet just five years later, a Ugandan agriculture minister was calling on Lake Victoria's shoreline villagers to 'strike back' at crocodiles he claimed were 'on the rampage': they should be killed, even eaten, he said, though unlike Kenyans, who regard crocodile meat as a delicacy, Ugandans traditionally shun it. The minister provoked the ire of conservation officials, who noted that crocodile habitats were being encroached upon – but admitted that crocodile numbers were simultaneously increasing.

These contradictions arise partly because the crocodile has long been so deeply integrated into the everyday life, language and folklore of African waterside societies. Amongst the Lega of the northeastern Congo basin, for example, the crocodile figurine or *kimena*, sometimes stylized as merely a yawning mouth or *kyasula*

overleaf: Nile crocodile basking.

59

kanwa', warns: 'Who does not stop quarrelling will quarrel with one who has the mouth wide open.' The *Mukondekonde* or forest crocodile (*C. osteolaemus*) appears in a number of Lega proverbs: 'Mukondekonde does not eat the catfish that are seated in their holes' translates as warning a 'junior' individual not to seduce the wife of an absent senior; 'Mukondekonde does not glide forward to where there is no pool' advises one, especially with regard to initiation, to address queries to someone of real spiritual authority. Initiation rituals are amplified by figurines, often amalgams of animals, carved or incorporating actual teeth or skulls, including the crocodile.[4] Among the Azande of north Central Africa, famously studied by E. E. Evans-Pritchard, medicinal systems and categorizations are complex and intricate, and utilize every imaginable substance in pursuit of cures. *Imangondi*, a fatal disease featuring deep ulcers all over the body, is known as the sickness of the crocodile (*ngondi*). If – it is believed – a husband strokes his wife's back with a crocodile tooth, any sexual violator will develop the sickness; so will a thief whose footprints are touched with a tooth by the property owner. The only cure is for the injured party to scrape some powder from the crocodile's tooth into water for the offender to drink.[5] In 1820s Natal, Nathaniel Isaacs recorded people nibbling crocodile dung as a charm against being eaten at river crossings.[6] Emil Holub observed the Marutse people in the 1870s cutting off crocodiles' eyelids, nostril coverings and selected dorsal osteoderms, exclusively for the king's use as charms.[7]

The crocodilian association with judgemental magic was recorded by a bemused Henry Morton Stanley on his epic journey to find David Livingstone in 1877:

A native accused of witchcraft was drowned according to doom today: arms tied behind, and a wooden gag in his mouth, thrown into a canoe and paddled into the river and tossed overboard. As he was tossed, the executioner cried out to him: 'If you are a Magician, cause this river to dry up and save yourself.' After a few seconds he rose again and was carried down the stream about half a mile. A huge crocodile, fat with prey, followed him slowly and then rushed on him and we saw him no more.[8]

Along the Zambezi, whose eastward-flowing, 3,200 km (2,000-mile) course has always harboured huge Nile crocodiles, an equally mystified David Livingstone noted another instance of

A heavily stylized crocodile carving from Zambia.

'witchcraft': a man could metamorphose into an animal, or have one as a 'familiar', and 'should a woman refuse him, he could send his familiar to kill her'. So, if a woman happened to be killed by an 'alligator', people would say 'that she has been doing something to offend some Morimo or god, or she is a witch'.[9]

James Stewart, who accompanied Livingstone on one expedition, tried to convince his companions that the creatures were 'true crocodiles', not alligators. Livingstone's response was, 'Humph!' Stewart followed up some (for the time) sophisticated biological detail with conventional prejudice: 'The *expression* of the eye was sinister, insincere, cold and at times almost hideously savage.'[10] Henceforth local beliefs began to conflict with invading Europeans' cavalier use of the gun and, in time, conservation efforts based on utterly different, ecological principles. Odd conjunctions and misconceptions ensued. For instance, in Nyasaland (Malawi) in 1953, it was momentarily thought that the carrier of sleeping sickness, the tsetse fly, was mostly feeding on crocodiles; it was therefore advocated that crocodiles should be destroyed. North Nyasa authorities offered locals 3*d* a crocodile egg, and some 8,000 eggs were enthusiastically collected along Lake Malawi's shores before the misguided practice was stopped.[11]

Traditional associations were also increasingly subsumed in global commercial concerns, for instance on the huge Lake Kariba, which dammed the Zambezi in 1960. Here both crocodile farming and fishing, both human and wild crocodile populations, have flourished, inevitably clashing. For some, the image of the crocodile has mutated from being the 'veritable curse' of African rivers, as one early traveller wrote, 'vermin' whose eradication was officially sanctioned, to being 'an economic and ecological asset'. This new view 'derived power from the authority of science, incorporated into national and international law',[12] but it has entailed the marginalization of, and exacerbated threats to, local

Nile crocodile, 1910.

fishermen. Netted fish, livestock and humans themselves increasingly become prey to attacks by crocodiles as National Parks protect them, the farms release legislated proportions of their breed into the wild, and tourists feed them from the ferries. Local fears are amplified by time-honoured magical associations, fatal assaults being blamed on humans practising acts of witchcraft (*bulozi*). Witches are believed to move around in the guise of crocodiles; and attacks by them are frequently attributed to older men, perhaps acting out of jealousy towards younger and more successful ones. A single crocodile death can have dramatic and divisive effects on a community.

Anecdotes of crocodile attacks along the Zambezi and tributary waterways are innumerable. One was related in the (then) Rhodesian police magazine, *Outpost*. A policeman, adopting the pseudonym 'Ingwenya' (crocodile), related, in a short article titled 'The Call of the Crocodile', the life-story of a Shona fisherman named Madungwe. Madungwe had in the early 1920s twice been savaged by crocodiles while fishing, having to have an arm amputated on each occasion. Reduced to utter dependency, he finally disappeared by leaping into a deep pool, insisting that 'the crocodile was calling him and he must go' – and indeed a crocodile had dragged him under. The writer 'was able to avenge Madungwe' by shooting a 'huge brute' of a man-eater, itself blind and wounded. The story is accompanied by a gruesome photograph of an unrelated dead crocodile with a woman's forearm lolling from its slit-open belly, just to underline the brutality. But the author doubted whether 'suicide, while of unsound mind' was quite the right verdict for Madungwe's demise.[13]

'Ingwenya's hint that there might have been a more positive spiritual element involved was not misplaced. As we have seen, deep pools are, throughout Africa, associated with ancestral presences, and crocodiles frequently seen as their guardians. Several indigenous peoples take the powerful crocodile as their totem, including the Ngwenya of Zimbabwe. Crocodiles appear in Zimbabwe's earliest rock art, apparently associated with boys' initiation ceremonies, as indicated by the presence of clay or wooden figurines called *koma*, which resemble 'a giant lizard or crocodile, doctored with medicines'.[14] Painted figures known as the 'crocodile men' near Lake Chivero, south of Harare, have

Crocodile rock paintings, Zimbabwe, probably associated with initiation rites.

been interpreted somewhat controversially as therianthropic representations of trance ritual.[15] Such spiritual associations are not merely ancient, but are constantly cross-culturally updated: in the 1950s, on Mozambique's Nkomati River, local Christians were charged with having sent a crocodile into the Sokotiba lake to destroy those who refused to be converted.

Associating crocodiles with spiritual power bleeds readily into political power, both symbolically and actually. Ancient associations are updated, so crocodiles are today habitually linked to the cold-blooded machinations of Africa's strongmen. It was always widely believed that Idi Amin, dictator of Uganda, dumped so many bodies of his political victims into Lake Victoria that they choked the hydroelectric plant at Jinja. A fisherman claimed to have seen bodies being eaten by crocodiles off the island of Mukusu, a 9.3-hectare (23-acre) retreat for Amin. Moreover, the obese dictator was said to keep crocodiles on Mukusu expressly for the purpose. But in the 2,370 pages of u.s. and British security documents archived for Amin's reign, there is only a single, dubious, third-hand mention of the infamous crocodiles.[16]

Hastings Banda of Malawi was also rumoured to feed his enemies to captive crocs; Robert Mugabe, president of Zimbabwe since 1980, has not – but he has certainly appropriated crocodile symbolism. The crocodile was strongly associated with the thirteenth-century state centred on Great Zimbabwe: a crocodile motif appears on the back of the famous soapstone 'Zimbabwe-bird' carvings, on a wooden platter found there, and perhaps even stylized in the chevron patterning built into the citadels' stone walls. Mugabe has propagandistically, though fraudulently, linked his genealogies to the Great Zimbabwe state-builders and their reptilian symbol. In *Mugabe and the White African* (2011), Ben Freeth, a British immigrant caught up in Mugabe's post-2000 farm invasions, links a scary encounter with an actual crocodile – which he describes as 'grotesque', 'ugly and evil-looking' and an 'absolute tyrant' – with an equally 'evil' Mugabe. He concludes, with breathtaking over-simplification, that 'Africa is in such a mess today . . . because the spirit of the crocodile has been roused by many of its leaders.'[17] Journalist Peter Godwin's plaintive accounts of white dispossession under Mugabe's rule included one titled *When a Crocodile Eats the Sun* (2007) – an allusion to a local Shona eclipse myth. Godwin averred that Mugabe's totem is the crocodile, *gushungo*, but this is not confirmed either by my Shona dictionary or any Shona Zimbabwean I have asked.[18] Tellingly distorted though both writers' views are, the point remains: crocodiles and power are consistently imaginatively linked. I happened to be in Mutare city when Mugabe celebrated his 88th birthday there in February 2012: the centrepiece was a cake topped with a huge crocodile in olive-green icing.

A wooden platter found at Great Zimbabwe attests to the power of the totemic animal.

Further south still, the Bavenda of northern South Africa associate chiefdom with the crocodile. Hugh Stayt, an early ethnologist, recorded Bavenda 'fear and reverence':

> No MuVenda [Bavenda] will kill a crocodile or take part in its destruction. If a dead crocodile is encountered,

stretched out on the river bank, the discoverer will push the body back into the river with a stick. He is afraid to touch it with his hands, as, if his action was witnessed, he would most certainly be accused of being a *muloi* (witch). The brain of the crocodile is thought to contain a strong and deadly poison, the smallest fragment of which, secreted under the fingernail of the poisoner, could easily be dropped into the enemy's porridge or beer, and would cause immediate and painful death.[19]

Some, regarding one's shadow as an integral part of one's being, believed that allowing your shadow to fall on river water made you vulnerable to being dragged in by a crocodile. But the reptile was also a guardian. Bavenda chiefs traditionally kept a protective stuffed crocodile in their sleeping quarters, and carved wooden doors, referred to in court discourse as *ngwenya*, bore cryptic crocodilian motifs: concentric circles for eyes, holes for nostrils and chevrons for the skin. When a chief died, the succeeding son would be shown his father's bones, from among which the *nganga* or 'medicine-man' would produce a small stone, supposedly first taken from a crocodile's stomach, which the son must swallow to ensure continuity and longevity. The Bakwena of southern Botswana also take the crocodile as totem. Some migrated southwards as far as Lesotho, retaining their totem even in that mountainous country where crocodiles do not occur; the crocodile is the centrepiece of Lesotho's coat of arms – appropriately after all, since some of the very earliest crocodilian fossils were discovered here. (A distant echo of that migration might be discerned in today's naming of the toll road north of Johannesburg as the Bakwena Highway.)

Not only black leaders attract crocodilian symbolism. The epithet 'Die Groot Krokodil' (The Big Crocodile) was coined for

Sign of the
Bakwena
(Crocodile)
Highway,
Johannesburg,
South Africa.

South Africa's apartheid-era president, P. W. Botha, capturing his
reputation for political ferocity. Doubtless under his regime arose
the macabre joke: 'How do the South African police catch a crocodile? Catch a lizard and beat it until it confesses.' Writer Peter
Wilhelm described that repressive time as living 'in the crocodile's
maw'.[20] Botha is alluded to by the huge puppet crocodile named
Niles featured in Jane Taylor's fine post-apartheid play, *Ubu and
the Truth Commission* (1998); the crocodile is staged as a predatory piece of office equipment devoted to shredding incriminating
papers. Botha died in 2006, and in 2011 his home in Wilderness
came up for sale, advertised as 'the Crocodile's lair'. Perhaps in
direct response to Botha's epithet, Gcina Mhlope wrote 'Spirit of
a Crocodile', the story of one Old Man Ngwenya (Crocodile)
whose village people are removed by apartheid bulldozers in
the 1960s. Old Man Ngwenya stays, and disappears into a deep
pool in the Ngwenya River, the dwelling place of the ancestors.
On returning to the scene much later, one of the old man's villagers,

Mkhize, stumbles on a piece of wood; it turns out to be a life-size crocodile that had once stood on the elder's veranda. The young Mkhize cleans and mounts it on his own 'stoep', in their dry, dusty new 'home' ironically named Othandweni ('Place of Love'), 'and suddenly he felt that the spirit of Old Man Ngwenya was now close to him'.[21] So here the crocodile is made iconic of the loss of both place and ways of life, of fertility and family coherence – and of tentative hope.

In short, the association of crocodilian ferocity and political power, actual or imaginary, is uniquely persistent throughout Africa, but cannot simplistically be divorced from more positive associations. This paradox surely arises from the particular nature of human–crocodile relations, to which the very real predatory potency of the Nile crocodile is central. Biology, to some degree, determines politics. Africa's rich legacy of crocodilian folktales, adages, magical practices and artefacts today cross-hatch in highly variable ways with modern and global governmental, scientific

Kipling's story
enacted in real life.

and conservation ethics. We can end with one of many possible
examples, that of the unique lagoons of St Lucia, KwaZulu-Natal,
the southernmost reach of the Nile crocodile's natural range. Here,
a burgeoning human population overfishes, introduces alien
plants (mainly *Chromolaena odorata*) and pollutes freshwater
inflows, all damaging to crocodile survivability. While biologists
intensively study the crocodiles' nesting habits, salinity tolerance
and interactions with hippos and otters, a nearby Crocodile Centre
educates, commercializes and breeds crocodilians, including
Africa's two smaller species. While local craftsmen sell crocodilian carvings inflected by almost-forgotten folklore, tourists have
to be warned not to swim there.

Here, as intensely as anywhere, tensions manifest between
age-old spiritual associations with crocodiles and modern de-
velopmental, commercial and conservation philosophies.

4 South America

Unlike in Africa, crocodilians seem to feature rather less in South American indigenous lore, political iconography and spiritual imageries. This may be partly because we still know relatively little about the scattering of tiny peoples who inhabit the deeper jungles of the Amazon, or they have been projected too rapidly into modernity to retain much of their traditional lore; and partly because (as one Amazonian river guide speculated to me) caimans are not especially dangerous. A sense of physical threat often seems necessary for the frisson central to the religious experience, and for an efficacious transference of magical power from animal to human through conquest or consumption. Thus in Brazil's museums of indigenous life and lore one will regularly find great necklaces fashioned from the more highly revered jaguar teeth, but little derived from the caiman. This is despite the continent being unusually well endowed with crocodilians. For reasons that may never become clear, the great tropical basin of the Amazon and the littorals of the Caribbean Sea have retained the widest variety of crocodilians of any region in the world: nine species in all, seven of them caimans. Some of them overlap in distribution; some hybridize with one another, disturbing taxonomic clarities. The ecology and distribution of almost all of them is only imperfectly known. This chapter will survey the various species before turning to some cultural history.

The Orinoco crocodile (*Crocodylus intermedius*) is one of the largest crocodilians, with males reaching 4.9 m (16 ft), and some unconfirmed reports of 6.4-m (21-ft) individuals. Its specific name refers to its snout being intermediate between the v-shape of most *Crocodylus* species and the straighter gharials. It is associated with the Orinoco River in Venezuela and Colombia, but has been found as far away as Trinidad and Grenada, presumably swept there by floodwaters and ocean currents. Its large size and attractive skin meant that it was hunted almost to extinction between 1930 and 1960: today, there are probably fewer than 1,500 left in the wild, suppressed by deliberate killing, nest-raiding, habitat destruction and perhaps invasion of territory by the common caiman.[1] Some hope lies in the fact that small breeding groups have been established elsewhere, notably in Miami, Florida.

By contrast, Cuvier's dwarf caiman, *Paleosuchus palpebrosus* ('bony eyelids'), inhabits a huge stretch of the continent, from Paraguay through Brazil to Venezuela and Surinam, and is relatively abundant, with a population estimated at a million or more. It is the smallest on the continent, very rarely exceeding 1.5 m (5 ft). Its diminutive size and 'poor' quality skin have saved it from most human predation, bar some subsistence and pet trade. It has the most unusual head shape of any crocodilian apart from the gharial, with a dog-like, raised cranium, a distinct overshoot of the upper jaw and backward-sloping teeth suited to catching crustaceans and fish. Its close relative, Schneider's dwarf caiman (*P. trigonatus*), or smooth-fronted caiman, is only slightly larger, and less widely distributed, possibly because it is less tolerant of cold. It prefers the shallow waters of forest streams, and ranges widely on foot in search of rodents and even birds – occasionally falling prey to anacondas. One 6.1-m (20-ft) snake reportedly died ingesting a caiman, itself some 1.8 m (6 ft) in length.

overleaf:
Dwarf caiman.

The broad-snouted caiman (*Caiman latirostris*) or tinga is the southernmost representative, occupying mangroves and marshes through Paraguay, Uruguay, northern Argentina and southeastern Brazil. A separate subspecies for the Argentinian population has been mooted but not officially accepted. Where this smallish (1.8-m/6-ft) species does not compete with its cousin, *C. yacare*, it is tolerant of a wide variety of habitats, temperatures and altitudes (up to 60 m/2,000 ft). Historically decimated by the skin trade, the species has made a good recovery to a fairly healthy 500,000 individuals, but, despite being secretive and mostly nocturnal, it remains vulnerable to opportunistic hunting and deforestation. Where it has declined, snails (its primary food) have flourished, carrying fluke parasites to local cattle, with marked economic consequences for ranchers. The slightly larger sympatric yacare caiman (*C. yacare*), taking its name from the regional term for 'alligator' (*jacare* in Brazil), has only recently been accorded full species status, previously being regarded as a subspecies of the common caiman. It has also been called the piranha caiman, either from its alleged preference for piranha fish, or because its bottom teeth actually protrude through the upper jaw. Like the common caiman, it has a well-developed covering of osteoderms, making it somewhat less vulnerable to the skin trade. Nevertheless, it was hit hard by illegal hunting in the 1970s and '80s; an estimated million skins a year may have been harvested from the Pantanal wetlands of Brazil alone. Though reduced to a wild population of some 100,000 and still poorly protected, aerial surveys of the Pantanal at least show signs of good recovery.[2]

Two larger caiman species remain. The appropriately named common caiman (*C. crocodilus*) occupies such a wide range of habitats and latitudes, from the Amazon basin through Central America and on to some Caribbean islands, that several subspecies have been identified or argued over. Of these, the most accepted are *C. c. apaporiensis*, so named for its habitat of the Rio Apaporis in southeast Colombia; *C. c. crocodilus*, found mostly in Colombia and Peru; and *C. c. fuscus*, the brown or dusky caiman, referring to populations in Mexico (though some argue these might be *C. c. chiapasius*). Since the common caiman (also called 'spectacled', due to the prominent eye ridges) has a high tolerance for salinity, it has been successfully introduced into Cuba, Puerto Rico and the U.S. It is notable for a limited capacity to change colour (metachrosis) through changes in the distribution of black pigment in melanophore cells – presumably a camouflage adaptation – and for its ability to survive long, dry periods, especially in Venezuela's llanos or savannah. Its ecological importance has also been ascertained: their nitrogenous waste benefits other aquatic species, so where they have declined, so have some fish populations. Underestimated, perhaps, is the caiman's niche importance, not so much as a key predator but as prey: barely 10 per cent of youngsters live to be a year old, an important source of protein for herons, otters, iguanas, jaguars, other caimans and piranhas.

Structurally rather different to its cousins, the black caiman (*Melanosuchus niger*) is the largest of the Alligatoridae. It has larger eyes and a narrower snout than most caimans, but sports the caiman-like bony ridge extending from the eyes down the snout. It grows up to 6.1 m (20 ft) in exceptional cases, capable of taking a capybara or even a human, and ranges from Bolivia to Ecuador, from Brazil to French Guyana. The number of human victims, however, appears insignificant. Some indigenous peoples, such as the inhabitants of Marajó Island in the mouth of the Amazon, used to conduct an annual hunt, virtually eliminating the caiman population there; and some Venezuelan non-agricultural peoples primarily hunted and ate caimans. Producing a shiny black leather, the black caiman was radically reduced by unrestrained

hunting between the 1950s and '70s. As a result, both piranha and capybara populations have climbed, with commensurate losses to livestock and crops. Though some captive breeding programmes have begun, including in Bolivia, much more needs to be learned and done to aid recovery from a low population of some 50,000.

The late John Thorbjarnarson, one of the world's most respected crocodilian conservationists, made the black caiman his special focus, primarily in the Mamiraua region of the upper Amazon. The Mamiraua was established only in 1990, through the efforts of José Márcio Ayres of the Wildlife Conservation Society, as a solitary, 1.1-million-hectare (2.7-million-acre) reserve aimed at protecting the fragile flooded forests from hunting and logging. Of this region, a nineteenth-century traveller such as Henry Walter Bates could write in 1863: 'It is scarcely exaggerating to say that the waters of the Solimoens [the upper Amazon] are as well stocked with alligators in the dry season as a ditch in

A caiman wrestling a coral snake, from Maria Sibylla Merian, *Travels to Surinam, 1699–1701*.

Opposite top: Spectacled caiman.

Opposite bottom: Common caiman.

A friendly black caiman, southern Brazil.

England is in summer with tadpoles.'[3] Passengers on early steam ships would shoot at the densely packed caimans for fun. Even in the mid-twentieth century, black caimans were regarded as abundant, but little was known about them. Rapid decline through hunting was followed by some stabilization, but even that, given continuing pressures, was somewhat mysterious – until Thorbjarnarson and colleagues penetrated less-frequented stretches of the varzea, or flooded forest areas, and uncovered some of the black caiman's secretive nesting habits. They were not so easy to find:

> As we skimmed at night along the edge of a lake in the Brazilian Amazon, the headlamps in our canoe illumin- ated a floating meadow up ahead. A medley of frogs in the watery vegetation clamoured at us with raucous honks. Overhead, squirrel monkeys chirped in irritation. Dozens of spiders clinging to stems of grass twinkled at us, their

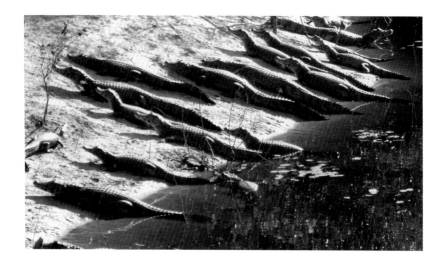

eyes reflecting our beams as tiny points of light. When we slid closer to the floating mat, the glowing red coal of a larger eye flashed back at us, and the outline of a huge black head materialised. Waves from the canoe slapped at this shadowy figure, and it sank into the inky depths.[4]

Pantanal caimans populate rivers and dams in their thousands.

Despite legal protection, black caimans remain vulnerable: the populations have become fragmented and genetic diversification slowed, though not to a degree which makes recovery impossible.[5] In a 2008 interview, Thorbjarnarson expressed more cautious optimism than he had just ten years earlier.[6]

Given this plethora of species, it would be surprising if the caiman was totally absent from South American indigenous expression. Theodor de Bry's somewhat fanciful 1631 illustration of the Tupinamba Indians brought back to Europe from the Amazon in 1552 seems to show the central dancers dressed in crocodilian-skin capes. From Guyana comes a typical 'origins myth':

The Sun god was distressed because his fish kept disappearing from his ponds at night. He asked the alligator [caiman] to guard his fish, not realising that the alligator was the very one who was stealing them. The Sun god finally caught the alligator in the act. He was enraged and slashed the alligator's skin, which led to scales being formed all over it. The alligator begged for its life, offering the Sun god his daughter for a wife. But the alligator was a liar; he had no daughter. When his offer was accepted, he was forced to carve a woman from a tree. She was not a complete woman and could not bear the Sun god sons. The alligator called on the woodpecker, who made the woman complete. A snake then emerged from between the woman's thighs. The Sun god accepted her as a true wife, and she bore him twin sons, founders of the tribe.[7]

In Manaus, the now bustling, central Amazonian city, I was told a local legend. In this story, twin girls were raised on the banks of the Amazon, one morally unimpeachable, the other

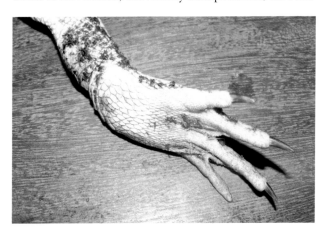

The webbed rear foot of a young caiman, caught at night on the Amazon River.

badly behaved to the point of evil. Jealous of the good twin's standing, the bad twin one day murders her sister, and feeds the remains to a caiman. When asked about her twin's whereabouts, the murderess lies that she knows nothing. As divine punishment, for the lie as much as for the killing, the evil twin is snatched from the riverbank one evening by a huge caiman, and so gets her just deserts. (This legend is illustrated in a scintillating painting by Brazilian artist Moacir Andrade, *O Casa Neca Manaus*, now in the Pinacoteca do Manaus.)

Andrew Gray's study of the Arakmbut, a constellation of seven clans amounting to some 2,000 people in the forests of southeastern Peru, reveals shamanistic practices analogous to those of Africa and Aboriginal Australia. In this society, Gray

Moacir Andrade, *O Casa Neca Manaus*, 1964, oil on canvas, illustrates an Amazonian folktale.

writes, the 'visible and invisible worlds interconnect in ways that parallel social relations within the community, and this accounts for the constant presence of spirits and soul-matter in Arakmbut daily life'.[8] The shaman, or *wayorokeri*, who can experience and interpret dreams conveying messages from the spirits, often appears in animal form, and can develop relationships with a particular protective and advisory species. Gray relates one such dream-myth involving the caiman (*mama*), which I paraphrase as follows:

A traveller found footprints of a caiman on a lake-shore, found the *mama*, and killed it by breaking its neck; then another. Then he cooked it. Looking for something to eat it with, he climbed the bank of an island into canebrakes (*wiwimba*); the *mama* offered him yuca. Thirsty, the man found sugar cane (*apik*), and slaked his thirst. At dawn, he continued his journey, finding two more caimans and killing them. By evening, he was camped in a stack of driftwood; a jaguar was calling, 'bu! bu! bu!', and coming closer, following the man's footprints. The jaguar started pulling pieces of driftwood away from the man's haven; the man started up and shouted, frightening the jaguar off, but it still followed him to a big tree where the man hid. The following day the man found, killed and ate another big *mama*, finding everything else he needed – plantains, yuca, sugar – and he bedded down once again amongst the protective driftwood. Suddenly something cold ran over him: a huge snake. He feigned death until it passed. Then he heard a 'bu bu bu boo!' sound, like a trumpeter bird: it was a call from Taka people, enemies of the Arakmbut. They discovered his footprints; passed by; returned; and went away down the river. 'Then dawn came and the man returned to his community, pleased to get home. He was a *wayorokeri* of *mama*, and the caimans gave him what he needed and helped him when he was in danger.[9]

This kind of relationship is explored further in perhaps the most beautifully written and self-reflective of all anthropological accounts of Amazonia, Philippe Descola's *The Spears of Twilight* (1966). Studying the Achuar, who live along the Ecuador–Peru border, Descola also encountered the centrality of the shaman, or *uwishin*. In a startling parallel to the African phenomena associated with Mami Wata (see chapter Two), deep pools are closely associated with huge snakes (here anacondas rather than pythons), a magical or ancestral people who live beneath the water (the Tsunki), and even with naked temptresses. Some animals can become the shaman's familiar, or *amik*, henceforth not to be hunted or eaten. One of Descola's informants related the story of a man called Yuu, a powerful *uwishin* able to visit the Tsunki:

Caimans in Brazil's Pantanal habituated to petting and swimming by tourists.

One night, he told me, a young Tsunki woman sought him out in his visions . . . She told him that her father wished to get to know him, to converse with him, and she took him down to the depths of the river, at the spot where there is a big whirlpool, enveloping him in her long hair. Yuu says that, in the water, the Tsunki have houses just like ours and that they are just like human beings in every way. The old Tsunki man was seated on a coiled anaconda and he had Yuu sit on a big tortoise that poked out its head to look at him with its round eyes. Other Tsunki were seated on a cayman lying alongside the wall and enormous jaguars prowled round him, barking like dogs.[10]

At this point Descola himself realizes the richer significance of various stools and benches he has noticed his Achuar companions using, one of them carved in the shape of a caiman: they are 'symbolic representations of the animals used as seats by the Tsunki in their homes beneath the water'. The same motif occurs in another myth relayed by Descola, in which the Tsunki appear as a single individual:

Once upon a time the woman Sua lived on the shores of a lake. One night she dreamed of a very handsome man and in the morning her heart ached with the desire to see him again. This man was Tsunki. Eventually, he carried off the woman Sua and took her to the bottom of the lake. There, it is said, Tsunki seated her on a cayman. The woman Sua was frightened as the cayman kept gnashing its teeth, so Tsunki gave her a stick with which to tap it on the nose every time it opened its jaws. Seeing that the cayman was becoming annoyed, Tsunki then seated the

Caiman-tooth necklaces on sale in an Indian village on the Amazon, Brazil.

woman on a *charapa* tortoise, where she felt much better. From there, she could watch everything at her leisure . . . The woman Sua lived with Tsunki a long time.[11]

Sua eventually goes back to her family on land and convinces them that she had indeed been in the realm of Tsunki, and therefore must be a powerful shaman; her family, threatened by

Caiman carvings on sale in the tourist market in Manaus, Brazil.

the possibility of sorcery, resolve to kill her; so she flees back to Tsunki and is never heard from again. As this story indicates, animals such as hogs, dolphins, otters and caimans 'play the parts merely of extras', in Descola's words, to the jaguar and the anaconda, which are also central icons in the Inca, Mayan and Aztec systems discussed later.

Given both the environmental commonalities and the great passage of historical time, it would be surprising not to discover both mystifying breaks *and* iconographic continuities between the great state-kingdoms of South and Central America (between the Incas and the Mayan-Aztec complexes respectively) and such continuities indeed appear to exist. One interesting crocodilian example from the Inca period is the Tello Obelisk at Chavin, Peru, which bears two hybrid monsters in profile, dominated by crocodilian features and covered by small plant motifs. One suggestion is that – as in some other cultures – the twinned caimans represent a 'complementary duality' – sky/earth, above/ below, material/spiritual – in line with the caiman's amphibious presence. It is nevertheless a surprising artefact, given that the Incas were a mountain people relatively remote from caiman habitat, though they may have traded in caiman products from lowland Indians, and even, according to one scholar, kept zoo caimans in custom-made ponds.

Still, in South America one finds less culturally significant crocodilian lore than diversity of species. The opposite is the case in Mesoamerica, which presents an exceptionally rich tradition of crocodilian-related art.

5 Central and North America

Crocodilians, naturally, pre-dated national boundaries and the names we give to continents. Hence some species spill from the last chapter into this one, from South America into the central isthmus, and from there into the United States.

The American crocodile (*Crocodylus acutus*) ranges across all three regions, from Venezuela, Ecuador and Colombia, right through eight countries in Central America, into southern Florida in the u.s., and across to some of the Caribbean islands. Like its Australian counterpart, the American crocodile is highly salinity-tolerant, inhabiting both brackish coastal and fresh waters – most startlingly, perhaps, in the cooling canals of the Turkey Point nuclear power plant south of Miami, Florida, as well as on the Tres Marias Islands off Mexico's Pacific coast. Decimated for the skin trade in the mid-twentieth century, the remaining 20,000 or so are legally protected but still subject to opportunistic hunting. Dubbed *acutus* after the wedge shape of the snout, they can grow up to 4.9 m (16 ft) in length, and are capable of attacking humans, though authentic reports are rare. One such report – rather redundantly termed a 'negative fatal interaction' in a 2008 Crocodile Specialist Group newsletter – concerned 42-year-old Alejandro Sanchez. Sanchez was attacked by a crocodile while fishing, as was his habit, in shallow waters near Oaxaca in Mexico: his lower right leg was severed instantly and he bled to death. Precise reasons for the unexpected attack remained uncertain, but the follow-up is not atypical: although a 2.3-m (7-ft) crocodile was captured and removed to Chacahua National Park 160 km (100 miles) away, continuing attacks on large livestock indicated that the wrong individual had been punished. Hence, three crocodiles were later found dead in the lake water, probably poisoned in revenge. Moreover, even over such distances translocated crocodiles have been known to find their way back. In Mexico's Chiapas state alone, authorities attend to some 80 'dangerous' animals annually. They have been experimenting with attaching magnets to the crocodiles' craniums during the transfer; the sample remains small, and we still do not know exactly how they 'home', but so far this innovation appears

American crocodile, widespread in Central America, but less well-known than the alligator.

successful. Their endangered status has inspired at least one appreciative poem: Barbara Helfgott Hyett's verse, 'American Crocodile', is closely observed, even spiritualized: the crocodile is 'Coiled in the egg, Buddha enclosed in herself'.[1] Indeed, there may be a less forbidding side to this already astonishing species. Several clips of a 'positive non-fatal interaction' between 'Chico and Pocho' of Costa Rica can be viewed on YouTube. Chico (real name Gilberto Shedden) rescued a young American crocodile which appeared to have been shot in the left eye. During the healing process, what can only be termed a friendship developed; twenty years later, the pair were still performing tricks and cavorting in the water, the now 5.2-m (17-ft) crocodile rearing up and thrashing its tail about with every appearance of enjoying himself.[2] This is rare but not unique: another Gilberto, 'Gil' de Magalhaes Neto of Campo Grande, Brazil, found his Pantanal wildlife tour business receiving an unanticipated boost when a number of wild caimans proved more amenable to human proximity than usual. For some seven years these caimans were happy to be cuddled by and swim with tourists, with nary an incident until 2002, when the land was sold out from under Neto by a corrupt politician. No one knows what became of the caimans. (Perhaps our conventional denigration of the 'reptilian brain' as merely primitive, instinctual and 'hard-wired' is simply wrong.)

The brown caiman, *Caiman crocodylus fuscus* (sometimes classified a subspecies of the common caiman), is another species whose range extends from continental South America across the Central American isthmus and (via artificial introduction) into the southern u.s. It has reached Cuba, as has the American crocodile: the incursion of both species has proved nearly disastrous for the rarest crocodilian of the region, the Cuban crocodile (*C. rhombifer*). Also called the pearly crocodile because of its characteristic yellow and black patterning, the medium-sized Cuban crocodile historically occurred in the Cayman and Bahama islands, but is now extinct in the wild everywhere but one portion of the Zapata swamp in northwest Cuba. Since an irrigation canal was dug through the surrounding hills, introduced *C. acutus* have been hybridizing with the Cuban incumbents, thus (as the IUCN website has it) 'threaten[ing] the genetic purity of the wild population'. Some would argue this is a chimerical objective, since sympatric crocodilian species hybridize in the wild anyway, and doubtless always have. The Cuban crocodile also hybridizes easily in captivity with its Asian counterpart, *C. siamensis.* It is classified as endangered, the 3,000–6,000-strong wild population threatened both by competition from brown caimans and habitat destruction, mostly by charcoal burners.

Another species, Morelet's crocodile (*C. moreletii*), is confined entirely to the Mesoamerican isthmus, occurring in Belize, Guatemala and Mexico, where it was discovered in 1850 by the French naturalist P.M.A. Morelet. Dark and smallish (under

Cuban crocodile.

Katia and the Crocodile, Cuban movie poster, 2010.

Katia and the Crocodile, Cuban movie poster, 2010.

3 m/10 ft), Morelet's crocodile is listed as low risk, with up to 20,000 individuals in the wild, but it is heavily dependent on conservation efforts, including reintroduction from breeding programmes in Atlanta and Houston. Overall decline as a result of skin hunting is thus being partly offset in some areas, for example the Sian Ka'an Biosphere Reserve in Mexico. Some farm escapees are even threatening other crocodilians, especially *C. acutus*, but in truth little is known about their interaction, and indeed about *moreletii*'s biology generally.

The ancient prevalence of these crocodilians in the relatively low-lying Mesoamerican isthmus ensured that they became well

Morelet's crocodile.

integrated into humans' daily and, ultimately, religious lives. From perhaps 9000 BCE onwards, so-called 'Indian' peoples settled and migrated through this land corridor. By 2000 BCE small-scale agricultural and subsistence settlements were already being interspersed by larger agglomerations capable of producing monumental art and the first recorded calendrical systems. Between 1000 BCE and 400 BCE the so-called 'Olmec' civilization flourished along the Pacific coast, laying many of the artistic and political foundations for the better-known Mayan city-states of the Yucatan peninsula (flourishing up until about 900 CE) and the Aztecs of the Mexican highlands (from about

1000 until the Spanish invasion in the 1560s). All produced astonishing architectures, monumental art incorporating animal motifs as spiritual icons, and highly sophisticated hieroglyphic scripts and calendars based on accurate astrological observation. In all of them crocodilians played a role.

That role is difficult to ascertain fully, or to generalize about, since we are observing its use over a vast period of time, with a great deal of regional variation, endemic political unrest and variable power structures. Only recently has much of the hiero-glyphic script been deciphered, not without controversy and obscurities, so that the precise meaning of, say, a crocodilian motif in the depiction of a religious ceremony may simply be beyond our present capacity to interpret. Most likely, what began amongst villagers as an animistic association of the crocodile with danger, power and the febrile underwater world of imme-diate ancestors, was over the centuries amplified into a more central mythic role in politico-religious structures. In the process representations became increasingly abstract and merged with sundry other animal motifs, most famously the jaguar and the 'Plumed Serpent' of the Aztecs.

Olmec iconography incorporated hybridized elements of mammal, reptile and bird. Each element no doubt carried a specifiable aura of magical association. Several scholars now argue that there have been too many misattributions of par-ticular features to the jaguar – or, as they call it, the 'were-jaguar'. For instance, in Hasso van Winning's *Pre-Columbian Art of Mexico and Central America* (1969), one clay figurine from the so-called Early Classic or Olmec period is surprisingly labelled, 'Figure with jaguar headdress', but even to the untutored eye the headdress is unmistakably crocodilian. Archaeologist and anthropologist Terry Stocker, for one, argues that 'the crocodil-ian may well have been a more central cosmological figure'

An Olmec headdress, often misidentified as a jaguar, is clearly crocodilian.

amongst many early Mesoamericans. Ecologically viewed, crocodilians would have been a far stronger presence than jaguars – associated with fertility, regarded as responsible for the arrival of the rains, and a ubiquitous nutritional and material resource. Quite possibly, too, in this formative period arose a persistent Mesoamerican myth that the crocodile is *the* originary creature, supporting the newly created world on its back and floating in a vast lagoon; and the central Olmec deity, sometimes called the 'Olmec Dragon', incorporates crocodilian features.

Like Stocker, Ernesto Pacheco argues that the crocodilian presence in later Mayan art has also been underestimated, pointing to Mayan lowland masks, presumably representing the central, composite and multiform deity of Itzam Na that bear crocodilian traits. Itzam Na was regarded as responsible for the great earthly and cosmic fertility cycles, well-represented by the crocodile's seasonal transition from water to land in Yucatan's intricate rivers and lagoons. Pacheco cites the great mythographer Mircea Eliade: 'the coming out of the water is a reproduction of the cosmogonic gesture of . . . regeneration; on the one side, because dissolution is always followed by a "new birth"; on the other, because immersion fertilizes and increases the power of life and creation.' Itzam Na was associated with the Mayan elite, who sought cosmological verification of their earthly power; so in his heavenly guise as Itzam Caan, the god was represented as a huge alligator covered with astronomical signs and his temple known as Itzamkanac, 'the place of the alligator'.[3] Material objects attest to the value of this worship: incense burners in crocodile shape found at El Tigre; a jaguar-headed human figure holding a crocodilian across its belly; crocodile-nosed oil containers. Most strikingly, the 'Izapa Stela 25' depicts the crocodilian incorporated with a flowering fertility symbol, which is sometimes identified as a 'world tree' or *axis mundi.* This same motif is repeated still later in the *Codex Borgia* from the Postclassic or Aztec period. In the Aztec Templo Mayor in the capital Tenochtitlán, a burial chamber was found to contain stone deity sculptures, incense burners and a crocodile skull; it must have been imported from the lowlands, testifying to both trade and its spiritual importance.

Little wonder, then, that the caiman or crocodile was incorporated into the region's enormously complex calendrical systems. *Pace* end-of-the-world prophets, who interpret one Mayan calendar as predicting apocalypse in 2012 (in which case you are not reading this), there are in fact several calendars, both Mayan and

Aztec, surviving ecological decay and Spanish destructiveness in fragments, referring to different forms of time cycle and still imperfectly translated and understood. In representations of the commonest, 260-day cycle, the symbol of the crocodilian, alongside nineteen others, apparently represented one day named Imix (Mayan) or Cipactli (Aztec), but what it might have signified is simply not known. That it was important, at least, is indicated by one Aztec representation of one of their 200-odd deities, Tonacatecuhtli, gesturing cryptically towards a stylized Cipactli-crocodile figure.[4] Alternatively, it represents a myth about the creation of the current age, the 'fifth sun'. The two gods, Quetzalcóatl and Tezcatlipoca,

> found the earth completely covered with water from the flood that ended the fourth sun. The giant earth monster Tlaltecuhtli ('Earth Lord'), a crocodile-like creature, swam in the sea searching for flesh to eat. The gods turned themselves into serpents, entered the sea, and tore Tlaltecuhtli in half. The upper parts of her body became the land, and the lower part was thrown into the sky to become the stars and heavens. Plants and animals grow from the back of Tlaltecuhtli and rivers pour from her body.[5]

The Aztec crocodilian 'world-tree' on the Iztak Stela.

Legends that probably originated in Mayan and Aztec times survived into the modern era. The 'Mexican folktale' entitled 'The Pujpatzá', for example, concerns a conflict between the sorcerers of two towns.

> The sorcerers of Ostucuán decided to destroy Tecpatán and all its inhabitants by flooding it with the waters of the Totopac river, which runs along the edge of the town. They sent a *pujpatzá*, the alligator that swells up, into the

middle of the river. The *pujpatzá* lay down in the river bed and began to swell until he became as big as a mountain. Then the waters of the river began to rise, and the people were in danger of drowning. No one in the town knew what was happening. Then the sorcerers of Tecpatán sent all the animals to find a weak spot in the alligator that swells up. But none of them could find it. The lizards, the little fish and the ducks went up to him and could see nothing. The crab arrived and went into the water, walking along over the rocks. With his pincers he began to feel the *pujpatzá*, scale by scale, until he found something soft – the place where the arms and feet begin, the armpits. So the sorcerers said, 'Let us make *juguetotoqui*, the fire iguanas, to kill the alligator that swells up.' Now the people of Ostucuán had built a huge wall between the two towns. They say that when the fire iguanas hit the wall, it blew away like a feather. Part of it fell on the farm of Pedro Gonzales Valdéz, where it still can be seen today. Then they hurled the *juguetotoqui* at the *pujpatzá*, and because they knew his weak spots, they killed him.[6]

Though there was doubtless considerable continuity between Olmec, Mayan and Aztec worldviews and symbolisms, they cannot simplistically be conflated or unified, spreading as they do over three millennia of turbulent states that declined as rapidly and mysteriously as they developed. Nor can the full spiritual significance of the Aztec crocodilian be fully penetrated, being refracted through the second-hand accounts of Spanish conquistador priests who laboriously interviewed Aztec laypersons with a view to destroying the very society they were recording. Despite the destruction of Moctezuma's great state, however, native populations even today retain many ancient beliefs and stories, and follow the centuries-old agricultural calendrical rhythms.

Further north, in the United States, indigenous societies survived European invasion only in shreds. So did their ancestral connections to crocodiles; together they were overwhelmed by slaughter and commerce. Eventually, paradoxically, American wealth also came to support extensive crocodilian research and rehabilitation efforts. The same generation of post-Columbus, militarized Spanish adventurers who destroyed the Aztecs established the very earliest European settlement on the southeast coast of North America, in 1527 at St Augustine, Florida. St Augustine now hosts the misnamed Alligator Farm, one of very few places in the world where you can view all 23 crocodilian species at once. Locally, of course, the reptilian scene is dominated by perhaps the world's most famous, and certainly the best-studied, crocodilian of all – the American alligator, *Alligator mississippiensis*.

Alligators once roamed from as far north as Maryland and Arkansas to the Florida Keys, but riverbank modification, notably along the Mississippi, and massive wetland drainage have progressively made more areas uninhabitable: the Great Alligator Dismal Swamp in North Carolina is no longer a swamp, and no longer contains alligators. Post-Civil War hunting practically eliminated alligators from lower Louisiana, and twentieth-century hunting throughout the southern states was only curbed by a ban in 1940 and the 1970 Endangered Species Act. Between then and 1983, Louisiana's alligator population mushroomed from 172,000 to 379,000; IUCN now estimates at least a million in the wild.

There were likely even more of these broad-snouted, forbidding but generally mild-mannered crocodilians in early human history, and successive waves of immigrants left their impressions. Of the first, 'Indian' wave, the Seminoles are best known, because they largely inhabited the lacustrine regions of the southeastern U.S. One Seminole village was named Alpata Telopkha, meaning 'Alligator Village'; the Euro-American town established nearby in 1830 was also named Alligator, until 1859 when – the story goes – the new mayor's wife refused to hang her lace curtains in a town named after an ugly reptile, and it was changed to the anodyne Lake City.

The earliest Spanish invaders encountered alligators, resulting in Theodor de Bry's oft-reproduced 1591 engraving of Amerigo Vespucci's crew despatching an oversized reptile with a huge stake in the throat. Sir Walter Raleigh's account of his search for the fabled El Dorado included an illustration of a 'Negro' being eaten by an alligator, foreshadowing the particular relationship between African slaves and crocodilians of later years. Africans brought their own folktales with them and in time

American alligator.

Baby alligators in a reptile park in Florida.

inflected them with local colour, geographical references and even medical lore; hence the tales of the trickster Hare of Africa transmuted into those of 'Brer Rabbit' and similar figures who had their brushes with alligators, invariably outsmarting the sluggish reptiles. Some Africans, especially escaped slaves, joined local Native American resisters to white rule. The tale of 'Uncle

Monday', told by Stetson Kennedy in 1942, contains elements of African spirituality. It concerns

> the leader of an African crocodile cult who, on escaping from slavery in America, became a medicine man among the Seminoles and their Negro allies, the Maroons. After their defeat by the white men on the shores of Lake Maitland, Uncle Monday retreated to the woods around Blue Sink Lake and changed himself into an alligator. 'He still lives in the Blue Sink, but every now and then he changes himself back into a man and walks through the land casting all sorts of good and bad spells on folks.'[7]

Amongst the early European travellers, William Bartram is undoubtedly the most famous. In his *Travels* (1791) he laid the foundation for a thoroughly unrealistic view of Florida as an earthly paradise literally bedevilled by alligators. Into this idyll, 'embellished with flowering plants and shrubs' and skimming teal, erupts the 'subtle greedy alligator':

Theodor de Bry's engraving of Native Americans killing alligators, 1591.

William Bartram
illustrated his
encounters with
alligators in 19th-
century Florida.

His enormous body swells. His plaited tail brandished
high, floats upon the lake. The waters like a cataract des-
cend from his opening jaws. Clouds of smoke issue from
his dilated nostrils. The earth trembles with his thunder.
When immediately from the opposite coast of the lagoon,
emerges from the deep his rival champion. They suddenly
dart upon each other. The boiling surface of the lake marks
their rapid course, and a terrible conflict commences. They
now sink to the bottom folded together in horrid wreaths.
The water becomes thick and discoloured. Again they
rise, their jaws clap together, re-echoing through the deep
surrounding forests. Again they sink, when the contest
ends at the muddy bottom of the lake, and the vanquished
makes a hazardous escape, hiding himself in the muddy
turbulent waters and sedge of a distant shore. The proud
victor exulting returns to the place of action. The shores
and forests resound his dreadful roar, together with the
triumphing shouts of the plaited tribes around, witnesses
of the horrid combat.[8]

Bartram claimed to have been surrounded by predatory alligators while canoeing across this same lagoon, and 'attacked on all sides, several endeavouring to overset the canoe':

> My situation now became precarious to the last degree: two very large ones attacked me closely, rushing up with their heads and part of their bodies above the water, roaring terribly and belching floods of water over me. They struck their jaws together so close to my ears, as almost to stun me, and I expected at every moment to be dragged out of the boat and instantly devoured, but I applied my weapons so effectually about me, though at random, that I was so successful as to beat them off a little; when, finding that they designed to renew the battle, I made for the shore.

With this lurid account in widespread currency, it is little wonder that alligators came, like crocodilians elsewhere, to embody both ferocity and deceit, as in an illustration from 1890 to a religious tract, showing a masked deceiver trampling on the truth, coaxed by a generic crocodilian into the dank waters of Atheism and Infidelity.

Settlers of French descent – Cajuns – who created a distinctive culture in Louisiana, also accumulated and passed on folktales of uncertain provenance. One concerns a certain bridge over the Nez Piqué; it was so wide that buggies passed side by side, and people liked to meet there. Strangely, though, cattle that strayed near it disappeared; and one night a man and his son swore that they felt it breathe beneath them. The bridge was alive. The town authorities dug, and discovered it was indeed a gigantic alligator, its head buried in one bank, its tail curled on the other. At night it unfurled and roamed the countryside, slaughtering. They lined up cannons, and fired ten times, and when they hauled out the dead monster the river fell three feet. They made 50 barrels of fat, and 50 pairs of shoes from its skin, and fed the army for a year on its roasted flesh.[9]

This tale is charming in its way, but symptomatic of that transition from awe or reverence to death by firearms and commercial exploitation. Up to the mid-twentieth century, alligators were hunted as vermin. Mississippi River folklore averred that the alligators were once so numerous that boats would 'run aground' on them, so they created 'alligator boats' to 'dredge' them; then 'they took them to New Orleans to the government

An evangelical warning against infidelity, symbolized by the crocodilian, 1890.

works . . . to make soldier-shoes out of their hides. All the government shoes are made of alligator hide.'[10] Probably nowhere is more strongly associated with the alligator than the Everglades. In those inaccessible and therefore lawless swamps and bayous, alligator hunting proceeded apace until government regulations began to bite – a transition captured by one hunter character in Peter Matthiessen's dark Everglades novel, *Shadow Country* (2008). In the 'great drought year of '98',

> Every alligator in the Glades was piled up in the last water holes, and one day out plume hunting, I come on a whole heap of 'em near the head of Turner River. Got wagons and a load of salt, got a gang together and went after 'em. Me'n Ted and a couple others, we took forty-five hundred gators in three weeks from them three holes that join up to make Roberts Lake in the rainy season. They was packed so close we didn't waste no bullets, we used axes. Don't reckon them buzzards got them carcasses cleaned up even today. Skinned off the belly skins, what we call flats, floated our flats down Turner River to George Storter's trading post at Everglade and got good money . . . it was war against the gators . . . Thousands of God's creatures was laying out there skinned and rotting before we seen that even gators can't stand up to massacres. The gator trade was pretty close to finished.[11]

The killing phase is not in fact over, merely domesticated, and it has been ameliorated by more widespread compassion and appreciation of the alligator's value to a functioning, wild ecosystem. Often, though, 'the wild' has come to include golf courses and swimming pools, as the reptiles take advantage of whatever water is available to them. In Charleston, South Carolina, I went looking for resident alligators in the ponds of a local cemetery and the residual canal systems of the rice paddies that once made the town's fortune. In this same locale, Gill Holland imagines the alligator's perspective, an old 'gator reminiscing on his victims:

> Watch the patriarch.
> Lidded, dripping, he awaits the statistical drop.
> He plays the odds like an ancient boulevardier
> with a gleam in his monocle:
> *Eighty years sez I win.*[12]

As numbers have increased, so have interactions with humans, though nasty incidents remain startlingly low. Between 2001 and 2007 there were just thirteen fatal attacks in the entire u.s., and only three or four in each of the previous three decades. An increase in clashes recently is largely attributable to illegal feeding, injudicious swimming or other intrusive behaviour. Even in this protective era, not many alligators reach a size capable of taking an adult, though there are unconfirmed reports of males over 5.8 m (19 ft) in length. The largest actually on record was a 5.3 m (17-ft 5-in) individual, shot at Lake Apopka, Florida, in 1956.

Humans more than get their own back: in most states in which alligators occur hunting is permitted under strict regulations. Following particular hunting accounts can reveal much about American culture – not all of it flattering. For example, on 16 September 2009, the *Los Angeles Times* posted a story headlined 'Florida Woman Bags 11-foot Alligator with a Crossbow'. Staking out a point on the St Johns River, 27-year-old Arianne Prevost 'placed two perfect shots from 10 to 15 feet and dispatched the alligator with a broadhead shot at close range'. Most revealing, however, was the follow-up in the blogs: these ranged from 'Will you marry me?' to 'The desire for people to kill is beyond me . . .

Alligator wrestling continued: Gatorland in Orlando, Florida.

isn't it enough that animals live in constant retreat from human expansion[?]'. Inaccurate but culturally significant prejudices surfaced: 'I love animals, but this is not an animal: it is a dinosaur / reptile that is as dangerous as a man-eating shark.' Hunters weighed in with their oft-repeated argument that they put more money into conservation than anyone; another writer equated hunters with terrorists; and so the blog deteriorated into *ad hominem* arguments and ungrammatical mudslinging.

The trite, often ignorant, but widespread attitudes so starkly evident here are not new: Prevost's 'conquest' inadvertently echoes an incident related in the 1837 *Crockett's Almanack of Wild Sports in the West*, in which a woodcut depicts a woman straddling an alligator, which is tied to a tree, and beating it with a pair of tongs – a telling precursor of Americans' passion for animal entertainments such as hunting and alligator wrestling. The latter continues to be performed in the u.s. and elsewhere, but it has lost some popularity as more educational and ecologically sensitive attitudes take hold. Even some of the more famous alligator wrestlers among what is left of the Seminole nation have recently desisted, such as Guy La Bree, last in a family line of alligator entertainers. 'Seminole alligator wrestling' began only in the 1920s: it was never a 'tradition' amongst them, but a product of the modern entertainment industry; and there are doubtless some fake Seminoles such as those fictionalized in Karen Russell's novel, *Swamplandia!* (2010), which is premised on the collapse of an alligator-show business. One website by the Animal Rights Foundation of Florida actively encourages you to write and protest.[13]

So America demonstrates particularly vividly the complexities of an antediluvian reptilian presence in a modern world. Alligators remain iconic of hidden, implacably wild dangers (even though, sorry, there are no oversized crocodilians lurking in the sewers of New York. Though the occasional zoo escapee *has* been found wandering Manhattan streets, the myth is just that – a myth).[14] Contradictorily, the alligator has been sufficiently trammelled as to become iconic of local, even national, character. Florida, with a kind of wry affection, has adopted the alligator as its state

Alligator wrestling, a rare postcard from Florida's earliest alligator park.

emblem. So has the University of Florida and their baseball team, the 'Gators. In this context, that most common question – *What is the difference between alligators and crocodiles?* – acquired the revelatory sharpness of the absurd when a university pamphlet provoked a vigorous debate. The pamphlet bore on its cover a 'large and aggressive-looking alligator' – except it actually depicted a Nile crocodile, 'a nasty beast indeed'.[15] Not only a taxonomic blunder: national pride was injured. As one (partly) tongue-in-cheek blogger put it, crocodiles are 'incomprehensibly stupid', 'deal drugs to kids', and 'bring ruination and despair', whereas alligators are 'outgoing', 'neighbourly' and 'incomparably superior'. The fact that alligators occur only in the u.s. and China proves, the wag reasons, that 'being a superpower is 100% caused by gators'.[16] The connection between crocodilian and political power is more attenuated here than in, say, Africa, but it is part of that continuum of spine-tingling respect.

6 Australasia

We move further west. Just as crocodilians reminded us that the Americas, including their islands, need sometimes to be viewed as a unified ecosystem, so they remind us that Australia, for all its size, is part of an archipelago of thousands of Indo-Pacific islands.

Saltwater or estuarine crocodiles (*Crocodylus porosus*) range from the Solomon Islands in the east to Sri Lanka and the Andermans in the west, from northern Australia to mainland Asia, including India, Thailand and China, and all the islands in between. They once inhabited the Seychelles, and individuals wash up in Japan. Their capacity for ocean travel is now well documented. One satellite-tagged male from the Kennedy River in Queensland, Australia, travelled some 580 km (360 miles) in 25 days, taking advantage of ocean currents. Another was translocated in 2007 from the west to east coast of Australia's York Peninsula. To return directly would have required an overland journey of some 113 km (70 miles); the crocodile instead swam north, away from its home ground, 386 km (240 miles) to round the tip of Cape York and back down the western coastline and home. That such travel has been regular and extensive, and includes inland freshwater locations and populations, is indicated by the relative homogeneity of the gene pool across their range.[1] Dubbed *porosus* for the bumpy callosities on the snouts of the

adults, the 'saltie' is the largest of all crocodilians, reaching up to 5.8 m (19 ft), with some unconfirmed reports of 6.7-m (22-ft) males. A one-ton behemoth measuring 6.17 m (20 ft) was captured in the Agusan region of the Philippines in September 2011, momentarily convulsing the world media.

The 'saltie', however, is not the Australasian archipelago's only crocodilian: it overlaps and sometimes competes with four other species of more limited range. Inhabiting the freshwater rivers and swamps of Indonesia, and marginally the littorals of Malaysia and Vietnam, the false gharial (*Tomistoma schlegelii*) is so named for its 'sharp mouth' or gharial-like slender jaw, and after the Dutch zoologist H. Schlegel, credited with its discovery in the 1870s. Since it is small and poorly studied, taxonomists still debate whether it should be classified with the Indian gharial or other *Crocodylus* species. It is clearly endangered, mostly by habitat destruction, and less than 2,500 are estimated to persist in the wild; captive breeding programmes remain tentative. Even more critically endangered is the Philippine or Mindoro crocodile (*C. mindorensis*), with probably fewer than 200 left in the wild. Small but heavily armoured and broad-snouted, it is confined to poorly managed and monitored freshwater lakes and streams on the Philippine islands, and has probably been extirpated from some of them. The New Guinea crocodile (*C. novaeguineae*) inhabits the neighbouring islands of Indonesia and Papua New Guinea. A shy, nocturnal animal, the New Guinea

Philippine crocodile.

crocodile is relatively well managed, both in the wild and in breeding and reintroduction programmes: the wild population is estimated at up to 100,000. Finally, a similar number of Australian freshwater or Johnston's crocodiles (*C. johnstoni*) inhabit the inland freshwater systems of northern Australia, generally avoiding the brackish coastal waters dominated by the much larger 'salties'. When overhunting reduced 'saltie' populations, the 'freshies' expanded their range; but the present-day recovery of the former is in places reversing this trend. Though ventral osteoderms make the skin less attractive than that of the 'saltie', they still became targets for the trade in the 1950s when 'saltie' populations were all but hunted out. Today, habitat encroachment and invasive species such as poisonous cane toads are having the strongest negative impact, but management and recovery are improving – not always to local human approval. One population in northern Australia, Adam Britton argues, might constitute a 'pygmy' variety, presumably adapted to local conditions.[2]

Both freshwater and saltwater crocodiles doubtless featured in the experiences and mythologies of the very earliest humans to land on the Australian mainland maybe 60,000 years ago. Aboriginal rock paintings, rituals and spiritual stories comprise an artistic and mental history almost as old as any on the planet. As among African and North American 'first peoples', ancestral spirits occupied every corner and facet of daily landscapes and consciousness; paintings and myths were not merely representations but were religiously energized portals into a communicable spirit world. In Arnhem Land, archaeologist George Chaloupka estimates, the earliest rock art precedes the onset of estuarine conditions some 9,000 years ago, at which point crocodiles begin to make an appearance on shelter walls.[3] Perhaps from this time dates a legend that some crocodiles, having grown too large, were imbued with bad spirits and banished to the seas, thus distinguishing the two species.

Unlike the relatively innocuous caimans of South America, Australia's crocodiles are ritually credited with the power and danger they really possess, and take a commensurately important place in recorded origin myths. Amongst Aboriginals near Katherine, Northern Territory, a myth is told of the Crocodile Ancestor, the only one to possess fire. The Rainbow Bird, who was subsisting miserably without fire and had been repeatedly denied it, one day swooped down to snatch up the fire sticks when the Crocodile was distracted. From the treetops he announced he would give fire to all men, and flew off, the fire sticks stuck in his rump. From that day on, the Rainbow Bird has always lived

Aboriginal wood
carvings from
Arnhem Land,
northern Australia.

Modern Aboriginal artwork, illustrating a folk myth known as 'Wilar the Crocodile'.

in the dry country, the crocodile in the waters. A variant on the theme from the Kimberley region, northwestern Australia, is connected to the Wandjina, a name applied at times to a legendary original people, at others to a single creator figure. In this version, a fight between crocodiles ensues for control of the stolen fire, possibly reflecting both freshwater/saltwater crocodile competition and human inter-ethnic conflict. Wandjina intervenes, sending a parrot to retrieve the disputed glowing coal; ever since, the redwing parrot has borne a scarlet patch beneath its wing where the ember was stored. The Worora-speaking crocodile that stole the fire in the first place is meanwhile stabbed and gutted, and where his liver and kidneys fell, great red stones remain; and this explains why the crocodile today lacks kidneys (in fact, they are just flattened and well hidden).

Such belief systems are not necessarily innocuous: otherwise-positive forms of social control can turn pernicious, or spill into manipulative accusations of bewitchment. Being taken by a crocodile can be interpreted as the workings of a vengeful curse. Some such grievance lies behind a myth from Maung country, in Arnhem Land. Some travellers came to Inimeiarwilam (meaning 'He pulled a bark canoe') on the King River. There a man asked repeatedly to be helped across, and was refused. Embittered, he thought, 'I'll turn myself into a crocodile [*gunbiribiri*].' Swimming to the other side, he found he was not yet a complete crocodile. He went to Aniwunggalainjan, upstream; he heated some ironwood roots over a fire, stripped the bark, pounded it into a wax; this he placed on his nose, to look like a crocodile. Then he swam back; the bark canoe was ferrying another load of passengers, so he capsized it and ate them all. His spirit rose and became the Milky Way; three girls he ate became the lumps on the back of his head.[4]

The enormously complex myths of the Tiwi Aboriginals of Melville Island, off northern Australia, reveal a worldview of history, artistry and belonging inextricably entwined with the natural world. Legendary stories support totemic belonging in very specific places, as well as explaining how things have come to be as they are. To take just one, a story from the so-called creation period: two men, Puruti and Jirikati, were spear-fishing in a freshwater swamp at Piper Head when they noticed, by the movements of water lilies, a large creature moving beneath the water. Puruti speared it in the neck, not realizing it was his own mother, Tipuru-undungu, manifesting as a crocodile. Urinating with the pain and fright, Tipuru-undungu rushed into the sea, polluting it with her blood, so that it became as salty as it is today.[5] These and similar tales are still regularly translated by contemporary Aboriginal artists into their characteristically pointillist paintings, often on bark in the ancient manner. Father-and-son team Charlie Matjuwi and Peter Datjin Burarrwanga represent the symbolic symbiosis of crocodile and foundational law (*rom*) of the Gumatj clan of Caledon Bay: striking diamond designs portray the analogous ferocity of the crocodile and the fire it mythically provided; others refer to a legendary fight between the crocodile and a stingray, which provides the basis for a Gumatj Makarrara or peace-making ceremony.[6]

How different has been the attitude of European settlers and their descendants: fear and disgust eventuating in slaughter and commercial exploitation. When the famous exploration ship the *Beagle* visited Australia's northern coast in 1836, its captain John Lort Stokes described his encounter with an 'alligator':

Every eye was fixed upon him as he slowly advanced, scarcely disturbing the glassy surface of the water, and quite unconscious of the fate that impended over him. At length he came abreast, and about eighty yards off, only the flat crown of his head, and the partly serrated ridge

along his back, appearing in sight. It was a moment of
deep excitement for us all, and every one held his breath
in suspense as I pointed my gun at the brute's head . . .
I fired, and never heard a ball strike with more satisfaction
in my life.[7]

The 'monster' was then skinned and appropriate parts eaten, the
flesh being judged 'not bad', white as veal. Even as a generation
of hunters set about eliminating crocodiles wherever possible,
some communities did develop a sneaking affection for certain
outstanding individuals, as Charles Eden related in his memoir
of 1872, *My Wife and I in Queensland*:

At sunrise every morning [on Garden Island], when the
water was like a sheet of burnished steel, a large log could
be seen floating under the 'big trees', which a stranger
would pass by unobserved, but which we, the initiated,
knew to be the 'Cardwell Pet,' a monster alligator, whose
favourite locality this was, chosen doubtless from his hope
of snapping up some unfortunate and thirsty dog for
breakfast. In this he was generally successful, until he had
devoured all in the town but two or three . . . He had been
fired at numberless times when Cardwell was first established, but now enjoyed a perfect immunity, and I am sure
the inhabitants would have been much vexed had any
injury been done him, for they had become proud of their
singular favourite.[8]

Such sentimentality remained relatively rare. Even by the mid-
twentieth century, when Australian hunting machismo seemed
to reach its swashbuckling peak, crocodiles were becoming dis-
tressingly scarce. Hence, among the dozen well-known hunters

profiled in Robert Reid's grimly enthusiastic book, *Croc! Savage Tales from Australia's Wild Frontier* (2008), some became devoted crocodile conservationists. Vince Vlasoff and Lloyd Grigg were the backbone of the Australian Crocodile Shooters' Club in the 1950s and 1960s, but when fashionable 'spotlight shooters' caused a catastrophic decline in crocodile numbers around Cairns, Vlasoff turned to opening a crocodile show called Marineland on Green Island. Similarly, Louie Komsic, who boasted of bagging up to twenty crocs a night on Cape York, reached an emotional saturation point: 'I'd caught a small crocodile and was about to put a screwdriver through his eye to kill him for stuffing later on. He looked at me and I couldn't do it.' Komsic tried to persuade the Australian government to curb indiscriminate hunting of increasingly small specimens, but for years was ignored. Ron and Krys Pawlowski, likewise shifting from hunting to conservation and commerce, setting up Australia's first crocodile farm at Karumba, Queensland, in 1965, found the Bjelke-Petersen government deaf to conservation pleas: 'the political attitude of the day was "if it moves shoot it, and if it grows cut it down"'.[9] Only in 1974 was legislation finally passed to protect both freshwater and saltwater crocodiles.

Since then, crocodile numbers have increased, as has human encroachment on habitat, with an inevitable increase in fatal or injurious incidents – almost all of them the result of human foolishness (29 per cent of people attacked between 1971 and 2004 were drunk). Despite the 'saltie's' reputation for lethal ferocity, human fatalities remain remarkably low. Even Michael Garlock in his informative but melodramatic book, *Killer Gators and Crocs: Gruesome Encounters from Across the Globe* (2006), notes that between 1980 and 1990 only eight Australians were killed by crocodiles, as against twenty by bees – and some 38,000 in traffic accidents. In the 2000s, attacks increased to three or four

Crocodiles are edible, but not usually in the form of a huge loaf of bread.

a year, partly because the crocodiles were growing bigger again.[10] This has prompted some calls for renewed culling: 'Shoot the bastards', Queensland politician Bob Katter fulminated recently.[11] But when a twelve-year-old girl was killed in Queensland in 2010, despite hysterical nationwide headlines, the general feeling was that the crocodile was hardly to blame.

A 5-m Balinese crocodile carving in mahogany, now at St Augustine, Florida.

A number of people, of course, have survived attacks. None has left a more eloquent, thoughtful or oft-reprinted account than the late Australian philosopher Val Plumwood. On 5 February 1985, Plumwood was canoeing alone in Kakadu National Park when her canoe, most unusually, came under attack from a large saltwater crocodile. Buffeted but not overturned, Plumwood headed for some overhanging cottonwood branches,

> and stood up ready to jump. Before my foot even tipped the first branch, I had a blurred, incredulous vision of great toothed jaws bursting from the water, as I was seized between the legs in a red-hot pincer grip, and whirled into the suffocating wet darkness below.

Twice, the crocodile went into the notorious death-roll – and twice, unaccountably, let her go. A determined Plumwood was able to clamber up the bank and, though terribly injured, drag herself towards a distant ranger station. She later mused on how in our minds 'we remake the world . . . investing it with meaning, reconceiving it as sane, survivable, amenable to hope and resolution . . . This desperate delusion split apart as I hit the water'.[12]

Investing her survival with almost religious force, Plumwood uses it as a way of thinking more wisely about our status in the natural world. She lambasts the shallow media frenzy, the machismo of *Crocodile Dundee* (filmed just three years later in the same area), not to mention a pornographic version of it called *Crocodile Blondee*, contrasting it with the idea of the 'common life force' in Aboriginal thinking, a power she invests in both the rocky Kakadu landscape and the crocodile itself. In a 1970 novel by Papua New Guinea writer Vincent Eri called *The Crocodile*, according to Plumwood, 'the creature is a magician: its technique is to steal the Other, the creature of the land, away into its own world of the water, where it has complete mastery over them'. In addition, Eri uses the crocodile as 'a metaphor for the West in his theme of the relationship of colonised indigenous culture to colonising Western culture'.[13] This reading, scholar Rod Giblett charges, has 'no real basis'; he prefers to regard the main character Hoiri's loss of his wife to a crocodile as a sacrifice to crocodile-magicians and the crocodile itself as a 'scapegoat'.[14]

In any interpretation, Eri is drawing on Papuan traditions reaching back thousands of years: Western modernity seems, as Plumwood suggests, both upstart and rapacious. The transition between them is treated in another Australasian island novel, Elizabeth Stead's *The Gospel of Gods and Crocodiles* (2007). In the opening pages, Stead economically charts a little island's history from its volcanic origins through the establishment of life, including mangroves and crocodiles, to the twentieth century, when missionaries arrive to transform the lives of earlier islanders. The island's origin myths, including one of a mother-creator crocodile, Stead portrays as originally one man's playful whims for the children; they nevertheless evolve to structure their society. One mad missionary is left out in the mangroves to be 'judged' by the crocodiles: they eat him, but his spirit is then regarded as reincarnating in a 'crocodile man', another immigrant named Sam Maitland. Maitland is honoured with a tattoo 'on either side of his spine, a design of scales', each of which, he was told, would contain 'the strength and courage of crocodiles'. His doctor insists on a tetanus shot. So values and beliefs smudge and transmute on an island one character glibly describes as 'Sea-base and crocodiles at one end, aircraft and crocodiles at the other end, sharks in the middle, missionaries all over the place'.[15] Crocodiles also feature as symbolic of indigenous belonging in another story of political transition, Robert Connolly's 2009 film *Balibo*, a rendition of the 1975 murder of five journalists by Australian-backed Indonesian forces invading East Timor. Early on in the film, an East Timorese elder tells a group of laughing children a creation story in which a crocodile rises from the sea with a boy on his back; his spines form the islands of the Indonesian archipelago. His village is as doomed as his traditions.

Papua New Guinea, among all the islands of the Oceania region, has received most attention. It is difficult to extricate one's view from the coils of European anthropology; but for this very reason the island provides exceptionally rich crocodilian material, including some of the world's most beautiful crocodile-related artwork. For most Papuans, no creator spirit is greater than the crocodile. Some Kawai people, for example, believe that their ancestral 'father' was a crocodile. A being named Ipila

A mask from Papua New Guinea, now at St Augustine, Florida.

once carved a human figure from wood and brought it to life by painting its face with sago milk: the eyes opened, the nostrils quivered, it made a noise like a crocodile. His name was Nugu; but he was not satisfied until Ipila had made him three companions. These men were recalcitrant, began killing animals, and became half-crocodile themselves: they could only make men, however – the ancestors of today's Kawaians.[16] Conversely, every detail of actual carvings, including masks, headrests, canoes and posts for buildings, carried significance. A wooden headrest of the Iatmul people of the middle Sepik area, decorated with baroque profusion, also has peculiar holes. The headrest would be placed in front of a ceremonial house; into one of these holes a 1-m (3-ft) carving of a woman with a crocodile head and a perched bird is inserted and moved back and forth a number of times, symbolizing the revivication of Betman-Gambi, a hero of local culture.

Of all New Guinean tribes, those living along the Sepik River have attracted most attention. Jean-Michel Cousteau described a Sepik initiation ceremony, one reminiscent of *muraiin* dances in Arnhem Land.

Sepik canoe prow, Papua, carved in a crocodile shape for magical protection.

About 4.00 pm the dancing starts. Fifteen men form a sinuous line representing a huge crocodile and circle around the *haus* chanting and waving grass pompoms . . . Despite the solemnity of the occasion, the dancer acting as the

crocodile's tail is the Sepik equivalent of a circus clown, whose elaborate gestures and comic antics make the women scream with laughter and the children hide . . . At 5.00 pm . . . the three young initiates, heads now shaved, are surrounded by their male relatives and friends. When the time has come for the last circuit of the exhausted dancers, each of the initiates and their male relatives join the crocodile's tail.

Once inside the ritual *haus*, what was represented in the dance is re-enacted with metal and blood: this involves the scarification of the initiates' backs with a multitude of tiny cuts, almost down to the knees, in patterns representative of crocodile scales, like 'an accordion of cut paper being unfolded'. There is a final dance around a tree adorned with a huge crocodile skull.[17]

Sepik society was penetrated even more intimately in 1985 by a young Englishman, Benedict Allen: he was himself initiated, invited into the 'crocodile's nest' of belonging. Allen was informed by a boastful Sepik Kavaak man:

We are Amwaarks – crocodile people – other Sepiks are scared of us. Of course they are, because when *you* [initiates] are hatched into crocodiles, we make life nasty. The Chambris, Palembeis, Blackwater villages – you name it, their ceremonies are pathetic . . . What's more, your crocodile marks are more extensive than any in Nui Gini.

Allen noted how crocodilian motifs were worked into their architecture, the sculptures of their great 'spirit house', the carved prows of their wooden canoes and the scarifications on their very skin. When the young man finally graduates, he joins a ritual dance led by a train of masked 'crocodiles', *avookwaarks*:

The crocodile slapped its heavy tail and shifted in the mud, bubbling and lolloping. The front of the fence was opened up. The women peeked from a distance as the dawn air cleared, and we manoeuvred in five flag-waving dances. The *avookwaarks* left us, fastening the fence up, to perform the dance of the crocodile, *kuta*, one time . . . The outsiders were wailing by the time it was dance number three, *kowook*. The *avookwaarks* walked out while the crocodiles rumbled again. The bigmen showed the mothers their hands – empty: the crocodiles are ready to take their boys away.[18]

So the initiate takes his place in a societal life and is regarded as integral to his natural surroundings, toughened and fierce and fertile as the crocodile. This is, as anthropologist Eric Silverman argues, utterly estranged from the image of Papuan life embedded in the Western imagination, which has been one of 'Hobbesian savagery, cannibalism, pagan rituals, and Rousseauesque ideals of sensuality, innocence and beauty'. These predispositions, accreted over a century or more of shallow misunderstandings, today still influence attitudes towards Sepik art as it becomes increasingly displaced from full ritual power into the trinketry of 'tourist art'. Still, Silverman suggests, even tabletops or masks produced for the tourist trade can express a reflection of new, conflicted identities, as crocodiles or snakes, already 'liminal creatures in the local imagination', are combined with others in new, individualistic ways. Such artefacts may be less mechanical, less obvious than it might seem.[19]

Yet one might remain uneasy, or feel short-changed by a mode of dealing with nature that, even as it funds its preservation, displaces an integrated reverence and mystery with entertainment and voyeuristic display: the crocodile less a motivating

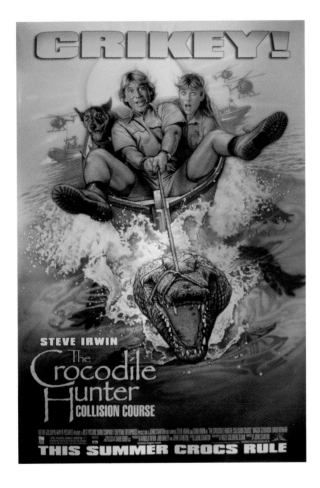

The Crocodile Hunter Collision Course, 2002, movie poster.

aspect of one's own being and more merely a biological captive displayed in an unnaturally transparent public pool through a foot of toughened glass. Even better, it is approached with appropriate frissons in a cage, as I did in Oudtshoorn, South Africa. You can do the same at Australia's Crocosaurus Cove in Darwin,

Steve Irwin, in a
Wallabies rugby
jersey, tempting
a croc in 2003.

where your putative predator might even be the definitive crocodilian movie star, 'Burt', he who nearly 'ate' the Linda Kozlowski character in *Crocodile Dundee*.

To conclude, then, by returning briefly to the Australian mainland: no one exemplifies the tensions between conservation and entertainment more than the late Steve Irwin. On the one hand, this ebullient Australian did a great deal to raise awareness through his reptile centre near Cairns and his *Crocodile Hunter* documentaries, even as many viewers deplored his invasive tactics and his propensity to trade on people's vicarious desire to come as close as possible to being bitten. When he once dangled his infant son above the jaws of his captive crocodiles at feeding time, there was an international outcry. On the other hand, when he died in 2006, struck in the chest by a stingray, the outpouring of tributes and grief was extraordinary. One poem responding to his death, 'The Crocodiles are Crying' by Rupert McCall, is clumsy and ambivalent (he calls Irwin a 'lunatic' but admires his 'redefining cheek'), but many readers found it particularly affecting. One wrote: 'Don't grieve for Steve: grieve for the animals who lost their best friend. Crocs rule!'[20]

7 Asia

Islands also stipple the margins of the Asian mainland, with which this chapter is primarily concerned, so by way of transition, here are two Far Eastern island stories.

One does not immediately associate crocodilians with Japan. Though fossil teeth have been found in Japanese Pleistocene sediments – and a new generic name, *Toyotamaphimaeia*, proposed by their (car-loving?) discoverer[1] – no wild crocodilians exist there today. One metaphoric usage is, however, both horrific and vivid. In *The Last Train from Hiroshima* (2010), Charles Pellegrino describes the fate of women and children who survived the atomic bomb blast of 6 August 1945 but had the patterns of chequered or flowered clothing burned into their skins. These survivors stumbled through the wasteland, being seen as 'ant-walking alligators' with 'their heads transformed into blackened alligator hides displaying red holes, indicating mouths . . . The alligator people did not scream. Their mouths could not form the sounds.'[2] Alligators are the epitome of an alienness robbed of language.

The second story also concerns the Japanese and the Second World War. In 1942 Japanese forces invaded the Asian mainland, sweeping down as far as Singapore. In January 1942, the Indian xv Corps spearheaded a counter-attack on Japanese positions on Ramree Island, off the coast of Burma. Outflanked by Royal Marines, the 900-odd Japanese defenders tried to link up with another Japanese battalion on the far side of the island – a march entailing 16 km (ten miles) of mangrove swamp and dense forest. There they were trapped, refusing to surrender, and there – the legend grew – they were mostly consumed by swarms of salt-water crocodiles. Naturalist Bruce Wright re-imagined 'the scattered rifle shots in the pitch black swamp punctured by the screams of wounded men crushed in the jaws of huge reptiles, and the blurred worrying sound of spinning crocodiles made a cacophony of hell'.[3] However, official British reports make clear, the trapped troops succumbed almost entirely to fever, mosqui-toes, drowning, hunger and gunfire. Nevertheless, the Ramree Island crocodiles remained sufficiently alive in the collective Japanese imagination to become the subject of a novel by Yasuyuki Kasai, *Dragon of the Mangroves* (2006). A recent book of *Guinness World Records* still cited the incident as 'The Worst Animal Disaster Ever', and American motivational author Warren Wojnowski was able to use it to illustrate one's 'self-limiting beliefs' and 'How to overcome them before they eat you alive!'. In an article published on positivearticles.com, he argues:

If 20 Japanese soldiers were able to cross 10 miles of mangrove swamps [on Ramree Island] and overcome thousands of crocodiles, while 980 comrades were eaten, I have absolutely no doubt that any of us can navigate the swamps in our MIND and achieve anything we choose to achieve.

Pity about the 980.

Aside from the littoral saltwater crocodiles, mainland Asia harbours four more species of crocodilian. Two occur, roughly, in the eastern half of the continent, which we will explore first. The Chinese or Yangtze alligator (*Alligator sinensis*) is related to

Saltwater croco-
diles range from
Sri Lanka to the
Philippines.

A. mississippiensis, but has bony plates, or palpebrals, on the upper eyelids, a more tapering and upturned snout and teeth adapted to crushing its main food – hard-shelled molluscs. Unlike its flourishing American counterpart, the Chinese alligator is critically endangered. Most of its lake and river habitat along the Changjiang valley, despite the designation of a 433 km (270 miles) reserve, has either been flooded or canalized for agriculture, so those that survive come regularly into contact with humans. As they seldom exceed 1.8 m (6 ft) in length, they are not a serious attack risk, but their burrows damage irrigation canals, their organs are prized for traditional medicines and their flesh is increasingly a delicacy in city markets. Farm-bred crocodiles are displayed live in Fuzhou or Xinxiang restaurants, prior to being publicly killed for discerning patrons: a foot, especially prized, cost 118 yuan per kilogram in 2009.[4] In 2007 police captured 270 live crocodiles being smuggled across the southwest border, apparently destined for leather factories. Public perceptions remain ill-educated and fearful, as demonstrated in April 2007, when an unattended nine-year-old climbed into an officially closed crocodile pond in Guangxi Zhuang and was eaten; military snipers took seven shots to kill the crocodile.[5] In 2001 the ubiquitous John Thorbjarnarson estimated that there were fewer than 130 wild individuals left, and that the wild population was declining at an unsustainable 4 per cent per annum.[6] Now the Crocodile Specialist Group estimates some 200, but realistically only very recent efforts at captive breeding by the Chinese government and others offer hope of survival: the

Chinese alligator.

hatching of 50 babies at Nanshun Crocodile Park in Xiamen City
in 2009 generated considerable excitement.

The second eastern Asian species, the Siamese freshwater
crocodile (*Crocodylus siamensis*), is similarly critically endangered.
It historically inhabited most Southeast Asian countries – Thailand,
Vietnam, Malaysia and Laos, primarily, spilling over into Brunei,
Indonesia and possibly Java. In the littoral zones it hybridizes with
the saltwater crocodiles, making identification and taxonomy
difficult. Little is known about its biology and distribution. It is
likely extinct in much of its former range, its skin being regarded
as particularly valuable. The current estimate of 5,000 left in the
wild is a crude one. Captive breeding, however, notably in Cambodia, has proved very successful: it was an added boon when
purebred Siamese crocodiles were unexpectedly discovered at a
wildlife rescue centre in Dhaka in 2009, affording conservationists additional genetic options.[7] Restocking efforts in Cambodia,
Thailand and elsewhere will depend on the restoration of severely
degraded habitats and on changing public attitudes; there are
some signs that this is happening. In Bangladesh, for example,
crocodiles are now legally protected, and in 2009 two men were

reportedly jailed for two years with hard labour for beating a pregnant crocodile with bamboo sticks. The crocodile, named 'Pipil', was well known and lived in a pond at Khan Jahan Ali shrine outside Dhaka; the men made money from exhibiting the crocodiles to pilgrims and apparently regularly beat the reptiles if they did not respond to their calls.[8]

Nevertheless, broader popular affection which might result in sustainable conservation is not automatically generated by the reverential historical iconography accompanying both species. There is the likely if attenuated contribution of the crocodilian to the legendary scaled and clawed physiology of the traditional Chinese dragon (a short-legged dragon was said to have appeared to the Emperor Fu Hsi out of the Yellow River). Pervasive religious iconography also accompanied the infiltration of Buddhism into China from India. Crocodilian temple carvings across the region, set into arches or the plinths of the Buddha's throne, show remarkable consistency across countries and centuries in their short, clawed legs, scaled or feathered skin and recurved toothy mouth – what is known in India as the *makara*.[9] The crocodile was sometimes depicted amongst the beasts of *mara*, deception, in the temptations of Buddha, as in a wall painting entitled *Calling the Earth to Witness* at Wat Chong Ta, in Ayudhya, Thailand. And it features in the creation myths of the 'Churning of the Ocean of Milk' – but mostly as a bemused and ineffectual denizen of the underlying sea, alongside fish, as displayed in the magnificent eighth-century carved friezes at Angkor Wat. In the words of the public display there:

Dragons in both Western and Eastern traditions had some crocodilian features.

Robert Robinson,
Chinese fisherman
hunting a croco-
dile (one of
eleven panels
with chinoiserie
decoration),
c. 1696.

The gods (*devas*) and the demons (*asuras*) use the serpent Vasuki as a cord wound around the holy Mount Mandara, which rises from the Sea of Milk. By pulling alternately on the serpent they churn the primordial ocean in order to produce *amrita*, the elixir of immortality.

An Islamic myth from Malaysia held that Fatima, daughter of Muhammad, created the first crocodile. Many folktales of such magical tenor persisted in Southeast Asian communities, at least until around 1930, when this Burmese tale about Ngamoyiet the crocodile was related by a villager:

Ngamoyiet was brought up by a Talaing couple in Lower Burma. They were fisherfolk, and one day found an egg in their net. They put it in a pond, and to their surprise they found a newly hatched crocodile some days later. He grew up, and they had to release him into the sea. But every nightfall they called to him from the shore, and he would come to eat out of their hands. One day he suddenly seized them, and, as the husband died, he prayed for revenge in his next existence. Ngamoyiet grew up and attained the age of one hundred years, at which age a crocodile could assume human form. Ngamoyiet assumed human form, travelled along the delta of the Irrawaddy, and at Myaung-mya he wooed and won a bride. But Nemesis was at hand. The old fisherman had been reborn, learnt magic, and had discovered the secret of the magic wand. Now he stood on the bank of the stream, which today bears Ngamoyiet's name, and hit the water three times, commanding the crocodile to come. The crocodile knew that his time was at hand, bade his wife and son farewell, and hurried to the magician, at whose feet he died. That part of the crocodile's body, which was in the water, turned into rubies, and that part on the bank turned into gold. But nobody could move them until the wife arrived. She built, on the river bank, a pagoda, in her beloved's memory, and died of a broken heart.[10]

Here we find encapsulated several key features of the premodern crocodilian presence: interchangeability with the human, mingled reverence and fear, the transitional deceptiveness of the amphibian reptile and the tight links to place.

Today, such religiosity persists, but in conflict (and largely losing the battle) with commercial exploitation, human population pressures and indifference or exaggerated fear. On the one hand, all too often death to the crocodile is the result of any emergency. When hundreds of crocodiles were unexpectedly liberated from a Vietnamese crocodile farm by a massive flood, soldiers and rangers were deployed to shoot rather than capture the escapees.[11] Better fortune met a 'rogue' 1.5-m (5-ft) crocodile, probably a farm refugee, that haunted the waterways of Hong Kong for some time in 2004, attracting tourists and even being voted 'personality of the year' on a radio show. Public responses to his capture ranged from sympathetic – 'Set him free!' – to murderous – 'A huge crocodile sandwich and make it snappy!' Similarly opposing attitudes attended a perceived rise in crocodile attacks in Brunei, which is heavily dependent on its water-sport tourism: while authorities responded by shooting a crocodile accused of eating a four-year-old swimmer (no related remains were found in its stomach), tourism director Sheikh Jamaluddin thought the attacks might benefit tourism by showing that Brunei's ecosystems were in healthy shape.[12] In a related vein, in Orissa and West Bengal crocodiles are actually being released into wilderness areas threatened by illegal fishing and habitat destruction, precisely to deter humans. Orissa's Bhitarkanika Sanctuary was estimated in 2007 as hosting some 1,400 estuarine crocodiles – one of which, at some 7 m (23 ft), was entered into the *Guinness World Records* book as the world's largest.[13] This echoes the nineteenth-century practice of both Portuguese and British incumbents in Goa, India, of stocking fort moats and other defences with crocodiles to deter potential invaders.

On the other hand, then, a tendency to leave the crocodiles alone is strengthened by religious ceremonies redolent with ancient ancestor worship. Pragmatically rooted in real fear and livestock loss, the 'Dhaus' or Goan paddy-cultivating farmers around the Cumbarjua canal continue to devise propitiating ceremonies. As one resident explains, 'The practice is done to

'Salties' are also popular in displays worldwide: this is 'Maximo', Florida.

Muggers are huge and ferocious-looking, but not exceptionally aggressive.

appease the ancestors in a hope that they would not let the fields inundate and destroy the crops, and also protect them from any sort of harm from the crocodiles.' In a manner reminiscent of West African *vodun*, it is not a real crocodile that is used, but a kind of effigy fashioned out of the silt from which the crocodile is regarded as emerging, with shells for eyes and white sticks for teeth. Where the stomach would be, a live chick is placed in a hollow, covered with a coconut shell, and left to die as a pro-pitiatory sacrifice. The ceremony is held on a new moon in the Pausha month of the Hindu calendar, a time chosen for its reference to the onset of the rains, traditionally brought by the rain god Varun, or the goddess Ganga, who is sometimes depicted as riding in on a crocodile.[14] Evidently, not all belief in ancient lore is lost.

So we move to the western half of Asia, which hosts two additional species of crocodilian. The first is the mugger (*Crocodylus palustris*), *palustris* meaning 'marshy'. The common name 'mugger' is derived from the Hindi *magar*, 'water monster'. Also found in Sri Lanka, Nepal, Pakistan and as far west as Iran, the broad-snouted mugger has proved adaptable to a range of man-made water habitats as well as saltwater lagoons. It was also once extensively worshipped as a servant of Krishna. Sufi Islamic devotees attend numerous shrines, such as that of Manghopir near Karachi, Pakistan, which boasts a 'mugger pit' similar to West Africa's crocodile ponds. The bandit Manghopir, the story goes, felt so guilty at robbing a thirteenth-century Sufi saint, Baba Farid Shakar Ganj, that he converted from Hinduism to Islam. His reward was for Ganj to exorcize the bandit's lice; Manghopir shook his head while bathing in a hot spring, and the falling lice turned into muggers. This reverence notwithstanding, it is listed as vulnerable, with less than 10,000 remaining in the wild, split up into fragmentary, genetically fragile populations. Restocking programmes began in 1975, but suitable habitats have diminished, so that there is now an excess of captive-bred animals. Thirty muggers formed the core of breeding programmes for India's premier reptile conservation centre, the Madras Crocodile Sanctuary, set up

A gharial's tail.

by Asian crocodilian expert Rom Whitaker in 1976. To date over 5,000 muggers have been bred, and the sanctuary houses some 2,400 crocodiles of fourteen different species – including our last and arguably the strangest one of all, the Indian gharial (*Gavialis gangeticus*).

G. gangeticus (named after India's great iconic river) is the last surviving example of a swathe of prehistoric gharial-like species which, as we saw in chapter One, may have been particularly important in spreading crocodilians across the post-Gondwana planet. The common name derives from the Hindi *ghara*, or 'pot', a reference to the astonishingly bulbous set of the nostrils perched at the end of the adult male's extremely long and narrow snout. Its interlocking, razor-sharp teeth are adapted to its primary diet

A gharial, illustrated in Alfred Brehm's famous *Brehms Tierleben* (Lives of Animals, 1865).

of fish; it does not have the bone-crushing power of its crocodile cousins, has poor mobility and is no danger to humans despite its large size. Males regularly reach 4.9 m (16 ft) in length, and some in India's Ken Gharial Sanctuary have topped 5.8 m (19 ft). The largest (possibly unreliably) recorded specimen, shot in north Bihar in 1924, measured 7.1 m (23 ft 3 in.). Despite a partial surge towards healthy populations after legislative protection and restocking efforts were implemented in the 1970s, it is classified 'Critically Endangered'. In Nepal, Crown Prince Shah Dev headed an effort to release some 500 captive-bred gharials per year into the Narayani River at Amaltari, beginning in 1981. However, an IUCN study estimated that only 7 per cent survived, and there are still perhaps no more than 60 gharials in all Nepal.[15] According to researcher Suyash Katdare, known breeding adults throughout their range crashed from 460 in 1999 to just 182 in 2007: at least part of the die-off seemed attributable to the consumption of fish contaminated with heavy metals and agricultural toxins. In addition, gharial eggs are widely collected for medicinal purposes, males are targeted for the alleged aphrodisiacal properties of the elongated snout, and suitable habitats for reintroduction and protection are eroding throughout its historic range. According to Rom Whitaker, probably less than 200 individuals remain in the wild.

That the gharial once occupied a more prominent place in human consciousness is indicated by one of India's most popular folktales, 'The Gharial and the Monkey'. This Tamil tale is summarized here following Linda Brookover's version.

On the banks of the sacred Ganges river one day, a monkey is eating apples so sweet they are called 'rose-apples'. A gharial comes along, and asks, 'What are you eating?' The monkey drops some fruit down; so amazing is the taste that the gharial visits regularly, and the monkey and the reptile become good friends.

One day the gharial takes some fruit back home to his wife. 'That monkey must have such a sweet heart, from eating this fruit,' the wife says. 'bring me his heart, I want to eat it.'

The gharial is appalled: 'But he is my friend,' he protests. But the wife is indomitable, and finally agrees to bring the monkey home.

The next day he invites the monkey back for dinn er, riding on his back. 'But I can't swim,' the monkey warns.

'We live on a dry island,' the gharial reassures him. Off they go, the monkey carrying a gift of rose-apples. So guilty is he at his ruse that on the way the gharial confesses the plot.

'Oh, it's my heart you want!' exclaims the monkey. 'I'm afraid I left it in the tree where I live. Take me back and I will fetch it for you.' Back at the tree the monkey climbs away so fast the gharial barely sees him go. Back home, he has to tell his wife that the monkey drowned on the journey – and never again do they taste the sweetness of the rose-apple.[16]

Indeed, recently the World Wildlife Fund has looked to enhance respect for the gharial by distributing flyers that quote the Bhagavadgita on the importance of the gharial in the sermons of Lord Krishna.

Finally – as we move westwards into Europe – one intriguing item from the westernmost limit of gharial territory: the ancient settlement of the Indus valley, one of the oldest human civilizations known and home to one of the earliest written scripts, Harappan. Translation of the Harappan script, consisting of 4,000 seals dating back to *c.* 2000 BCE, is often regarded as well-nigh impossible. However, the combination of signs and often start-lingly realistic animal relief carvings offer some clues. The animal on each seal is usually a long-horned bull, but also include zebus, water buffaloes, goats, tigers, elephants – and gharials. Some seals bear animal groups apparently presided over by an anthropomorphic figure dubbed 'Lord of the Beasts', sometimes wearing an animal mask. Above several groups appears the gharial, in one case with a recognizable fish in front of its snout.[17] Quite what this means remains shrouded in some obscurity, but it seems safe to speculate that we are observing here traces of an animistic mindset not unlike those we have encountered in Africa, Central America and Aboriginal Australasia, with a

The Hindu goddess Maiya on a crocodile.

shamanistic figure at the centre of a totemistic use of animal-spiritual powers. In European iconography, by contrast, the absence of resident crocodiles and the advent of scientific and imperial modernity there generated quite different attitudes.

8 Europe

When Alexander the Great reached the Indus River in 326 BCE, he encountered crocodiles – whether gharials or muggers is not recorded. Crocodiles and Egypt were already so firmly wedded in the European imagination that he temporarily mistook the Indus for the Nile. He may have sent specimens back, as was his wont on his imperialistic adventures, to his great mentor Aristotle, who could then incorporate the information into his foundational survey of animal types, *Historia Animalium*. Almost certainly Alexander's successors, the Ptolemys, made a spectacle of crocodiles in their pageants and collections – amongst the first recorded animal zoos. In the centuries after Alexander, many southern Europeans travelled between the Mediterranean world and India, but few, it seems, contributed much to knowledge of Asian crocodilians. Subsequent writers, pre-eminently Porphyry, Strabo and Pliny, were content rather to repeat what Herodotus and Aristotle had written, including some of their more astonishing misconceptions. This is strange, given that the Roman Empire stretched from Egypt to Britain, and live crocodiles were tortured in Roman arenas up to the second century CE. These martyrs to entertainment almost certainly originated in Egypt. In 112 BCE, the advent of the Roman senator in the Fayum, the heart of Egyptian crocodile worship, prompted the despatch of a papyrus memo to local authorities to give him a 'magnificent reception', including 'the

tidbits for Petesouchos and the crocodiles' – Petesouchos being
the tame sacred crocodile, doubtless the ancestor of the one visited
by Strabo in the time of Christ:

> Our host, a man of position who took us around there,
> went out to the lake and took with him from dinner a bis-
> cuit, some roast meat, and a jug of honey and wine. We
> found the crocodile lying on the bank. The priests went
> up to him, and while some held his mouth open, another
> put in the biscuit, next the meat, and then poured down
> the wine. The crocodile plunged into the lake and swam
> to the other side.[1]

Swam a little erratically, no doubt.

Despite touristic contacts like Strabo's, for a good millennium
Europeans' depictions remained comprehensively insulated from
the living creature. So far we have seen, almost everywhere else on
the planet, indigenous societies integrating reality-based crocodilia into everyday and spiritual life. In Europe, in contrast, the
crocodile assumes ever more complex, intellectualized and attenuated status as an emblem of moralistic, largely Christian, allegory.

154

Only in the late eighteenth century does a more scientific, realistic view of crocodilians, supported by the increasing importation of live and dead animals from expanding imperial conquests, begin to usurp the fantastical tradition.

Take just one exemplary misconception. Herodotus asserted that the crocodile had no tongue, and that it moved the upper jaw, the lower being fixed. Aristotle correctly declared that there is an inconspicuous tongue, but he repeated the misinformation about the lower jaw's immobility. Pliny, in the first century CE, recycled both misconceptions; as did Isidore of Seville in his *Etymologies* of the seventh century, Guillaume le Clerc in his thirteenth-century *Bestiare* and the wholly unreliable Sir John Mandeville in his *Travels* a century after that. This matter of the jaw was bought to bear on the identification of the biblical

Pavement mosaic of a Nile scene, Maccarani Vineyard, Rome, *c.* 2nd century.

Leviathan (attached to crocodiles as much as to whales in popular imaginations and exegetical argument alike). By 1666, commentators like Joseph Caryl were attempting to reconcile biblical and Classical sources. Caryl noted that the second half of Job 41.1

> is made use of by some, as an argument to prove that Leviathan cannot be the Crocodile, who, as Naturalists write of him, hath no tongue; his mouth is wide, but tongueless. To this objection, *Beza* gives one, and *Bocharius* [Bochart] adds a second answer. The former saith, it is not strictly affirmed in the Text, that Leviathan hath a tongue; 'tis only denied, that he hath a tongue in which a cord or hook may be fastned. The latter saith, that the Crocodile is not altogether *tongue-less*, but only (as we speak of it in another sense) *tongue-tied*. He hath a tongue, but 'tis an immoveable one, cleaving fast to his lower jaw.[2]

Among the seventeenth-century poets, these features assume the quality of purely playful metaphor. Robert Herrick depicts an abashed lover standing 'mute the while, / As is the fish, or tonguelesse Crocadile'; and, compressing it into Christian allegory, George Herbert uses the crocodile's allegedly unique jaw structure to argue that God is not bound by the 'shibboleth of consistency': 'Most things move th' under-jaw; the Crocodile not.'

We have already encountered the myth of the crocodile's tears, which also transmuted into a Christianized image of hypocrisy. In representations spanning the dark centuries between the fall of the Roman empire and the reintroduction of Classical texts via the Arabs in the early medieval period, the crocodile becomes synthesized out of sundry sources as the ultimate beast of hypocritical evil – a veritable dragon to be slain, or at least tamed.

Egyptian, Classical, pre-Roman Celtic and Gallic sources fed into Christian lore in ways which still often remain obscure. For example, a mural uncovered from the lava flows of Pompeii shows a scene of dark, bulbous-headed 'pygmies', apparently both being attacked by and catching crocodiles, even riding a reined one. Walton Brooks McDaniel argued in 1932 that these 'pygmies' were the Tentyritae people, mentioned by both Pliny and Strabo as 'especially famed for their presence of mind in

A tiny figure in painted lead continues the artistic theme of crocodilian predation on black children.

A crocodile and hippo hunt on the Nile, depicted on a Pompeii mural.

assailing the crocodile'.[3] This fresco's creatures are premonitory of the distorted, sharp-nosed depictions in later medieval bestiaries. Similarly, in another, positively graphic Pompeiian mural depicting lovers on a Nile boat apparently under siege by two crocodiles, the reptiles have pointed, extended upper noses and thin, lizard-like tails. This retention of both Egyptian mythic elements and artistic motifs becomes just one strand in the complex formation of the symbolic crocodilian presence in the European mind.

Linguistic historian Alice Miskimin has tracked one extraordinary line of this syncretic form of allegory. A widespread cult of the virginal St Marte took hold in Europe in the thirteenth

ft animal in nilo flumine qd dicit ydrū in aqua

century; her emblematic attribute was the crocodile. St Marte's antecedents included the Egyptian figure of Isis, suckled by snakes; the Cretan goddess Britomartis, or Artemis, with her ability to subdue wild animals, introduced by Greek colonies to Gaul in the first century CE; pre-Roman Celtic myths of the dragon-like *tarasque* of the Rhône, said to have terrorized farmers and fishermen and devoured cattle; and the semi-legendary Merovingian queen St Radegunde, who slew the *draco*, an amphibious 'demon' described in Philippe de Thaun's *Bestiary* of 1125 as 'Crocodrille, signifie diable en cest vie'. Retrospectively, church commentators would conflate these figures with the biblical Martha of Bethany. In some legends, after Jesus's death certain vengeful Jews set Martha adrift in a boat on the Mediterranean, along with Mary Magdalene and Lazarus. Ultimately lodging in

Illuminated manuscript, England, c. 1230–40. A crocodile devouring a hydra.

a contemplative's cave near Aix, France, the virginal lady executed her signature miracle of quelling the dragon simply by invoking Christ. St Martha's nineteenth-century hagiographer, the Abbé Faillon, had 'no doubt that the Tarasque or dragon which S. Martha subdued was a crocodile from Egypt'; how it got to France, he does not explain. At any rate, the final version of St Marte (Martha) came to be conventionally displayed crowned, the crocodile supine at her feet but often, ambiguously, with its tail reaching upward to embrace her waist.[4]

This ambiguity – a hint of the sensual brushing against the assertion of divinely sanctioned chastity – is deepened in Edmund Spenser's great Christian epic poem, *The Faerie Queene*. Spenser, in creating one of several central quest figures, Britomart, drew on many of these legends and sources while synthesizing them with still other literary parallels, such as that in Ariosto's *Orlando Furioso* (1532):

> The Necromancer fought with vantage great,
> He rode upon a cruell hideous beast,
> A Crocodile that flesh of men doth eat,
> And birds and beast, and doth them all digest . . . (51)

In Book v of *The Faerie Queene*, Spenser first portrays Britomart experiencing a dream at the Temple of Isis, strongly echoing St Martha in her guise of Prudence personified:

> Uponn her head she wore a Crowne of gold,
> To shew that she had powre in things divine;
> And at her feete a Crocodile was rold,
> That with her wreathed taile her middle did enfold.
> . . . One foot was set upon the Crocodile,
> And on the ground the other fast did stand,

So meaning to suppresse both forged guile
And open force . . . (v.vii.6–7)

Hypocrisy and physical power, both long associated with the crocodile, are here subjected to divinely sanctioned authority. When Britomart sacrifices to Isis, the crocodile at her feet 'seem'd to wake in horrible dismay', accompanied by high winds and fire representing 'both life-saving strength and devouring masculine energy'. Britomart finally inspires the crocodile to turn 'all his pride to humblenesse meek', but he is ultimately neither slain nor chaste: unlike Isis, Martha and the other antecedent virgins, Britomart will bear a child – as Spenser hoped his real Queen Elizabeth, to whom the epic is dedicated, would also do. The crocodile has become, startlingly, part of God's blessing and fecund 'joyance'.[5]

The literary line of influence exemplified by Spenser's case unfolded against a background of crocodilian or variously dragon-like representations throughout Europe. Skeletons and skins of crocodiles were displayed like sundry other monstrosities and gargoyles on the cornices of medieval churches. A primary textual source was the *Physiologus*, reputed to have been compiled in Alexandria in the second century. Derivative medieval bestiaries thereafter regularly included wildly inaccurate crocodiles and invented part-crocodilian creatures such as gryphons and wyverns. The 'Arabian or Egyptian crocodile' depicted in a woodcut in Conrad Gessner's *Historia Animalium* (1551) looks more like a spiny lizard. Erhard Reuwich's 'Crocodillus' in his 1486 *Perigrinationes ad Terram Sanctum* has the coiling serpentine tail and extended neck of a dragon. These visual depictions were often accompanied by textual homilies to virtue: 'Hypocritical, dissolute and avaricious people have the same nature as this brute – also any people who are puffed up with the vice of pride, dirtied

Conrad Gessner's conception of an 'Arabian Crocodile', 1551, illustration.

with the corruption of luxury, or haunted with the disease of avarice.' In some, the ephemeral quality of earthbound vanity is signified by crocodile dung, from which is made 'an ointment with which old women and faded whores anoint their faces, and appear beautiful until their sweat washes it off'.[6] Good for hair-loss, too.

Another groundless but oft-repeated legend was that of the hate-filled 'rat of India' – the 'ichneumon' or mongoose. According to Pliny, when the trochilus bird has done its dental work and the crocodile has fallen asleep with its mouth agape, the ichneumon – as one sixteenth-century translation puts it – 'Into the Tirants greedie gorge doth flie / And feeds upon that Glutton', eating its way out through the side. In some texts, the ichneumon mutates into a 'hydrus' (not to be confused with the hydra), a serpent-like creature which likewise would coat itself with slimy mud, plunge into the crocodile's unwary maw, and burst its way out through the stomach. This, too, came to have Christian allegorical significance: the crocodiles were said to represent death and hell, and the hydrus Christ. The hydrus enters the

crocodile's maw, like Christ entering Hell, then bursts out in a kind of resurrection, overcoming death and liberating those unjustly imprisoned. Finally, the crocodile's allegorically impenetrable hide could be invoked in quite contradictory ways. In Christopher Marlowe's Renaissance play *Tamburlaine the Great* (1590), it is an image of the cowardice of 'faint-hearted base Egyptians' who 'lie slumbering on the flow'ry banks of Nile / As crocodiles that unaffrighted rest / While thund'ring cannons rattle on their skins' (1.iv.1). In contrast, for the seventeenth-century English poet George Wither the same hide is a 'coate of Maile' emblematic of the impenetrability of 'True Vertue'.[7] And where Spenser had regarded the amphibious nature of the crocodile as 'monstrous', as part of the 'strange ayde' which supports tyranny, the angel Raphael's Edenic crocodile in John Milton's *Paradise Lost* (1671) is more matter-of-factly naturalistic, following Aristotle in being primarily fascinated by the category-defying nature of amphibians like 'The River Horse [hippopotamus] and scalie Crocodile' (7.474). By this time, European exploratory ventures had encountered real alligators in the Americas and crocodiles in West Africa, and Milton himself may have been able to stroke bits of alligator hide displayed in London at Tradescant's Ark, South Lambeth. (Yet the Christian moralism would continue overtly at least until John Ruskin who, trying to counter Darwin in 1869, called crocodiles 'words of God' representing the ultimate state of 'moral evil'.)

The beginnings of global exploration were also stimulating the popularity, especially among wealthy merchants, of 'cabinets of curiosity' – proto-museums which gathered the most bizarre-seeming natural objects from around the world, arranged densely in idiosyncratic ways. The earliest church collections, such as St Denis in France, were amplified by 'enlightened collectors [who] preferred the immutable and unchanging nature of objects to the illusions of a world in a constant state of flux' and who were 'united by a dogged and undeviating determination to compress the contents of an entire library into a single volume'. Among many Baroque-period collectors – including John Tradescant and Elias Ashmole in Oxford, still others in Milan, Paris, Aix-en-Provence, Worms, Basle, Zurich and Halle, the last being where August Hermann Francke began the best-preserved collection, the *Kunst und Naturalienkammer* in 1598 – it became almost de rigueur for a stuffed crocodile to assume pride of place, suspended from the ceiling.[8]

Despite this increasing availability of real crocodiles for viewing, the artistic conventions established in medieval times continued to appear for another century or more. Marten de Vos's depiction, engraved by Adriaen Collaert in the late 1500s, is of a semi-mythical, animal-populated Africa, the central creature being a reasonably naturalistic crocodile ridden by a naked woman. Pretty accurate, if couched in riotous visual melodrama, is the crocodile depicted in *Hippopotamus and Crocodile Hunt* (1616) by Peter Paul Rubens. On the other hand, the crocodile in Johann Michael Zinck's painting of 1741 in the church of St Sebastian in Wolframs-Eschenbach, Germany, is still medievally sharp-nosed, with an undershot jaw and a distinctly visible tongue.

Crocodiles held pride of place in early cabinets of curiosities; the museum of Ferrante Imperato, Naples, 1599.

This painting, an allegory for the sturdiness of faith, shows the virtuous Christian shielding himself from the crocodile and a prancing gryphon with the words, *Ne terreamini ab his* (Be not afraid of these); a crude pyramid in the background alludes to the monsters' origins in Egypt. An image from *The Travels and Surprising Adventures of Baron Munchausen* (1793), likewise depicted a very unrealistic, straight-jawed crocodile attempting to swallow a lion while the intrepid baron raises his sword above them, preparatory to beheading both at once and making trophies of them.

Just five years later, Napoleon Bonaparte invaded Egypt, and adopted the crocodile, suitably chained to a palm tree, as the motif of his conquest; he embossed it on commemorative medals consciously echoing those of the Roman emperor Augustus. (The French town of Nîmes still uses this image on its flag and escutcheon, since veterans of Julius Caesar's Egyptian campaigns were allocated land there. Nîmes is full of crocodile representations, including Alexandre Falguière's sculpture of 1900 in the central market place, and four suspended from the corners of the ceiling of the Hôtel de Ville, designed by Albin Michel in 1876.) English caricaturists seized on Napoleon's hubris to deride *his* campaign: James Gillray depicted a Frenchman futilely trying to bridle and ride the Egyptian crocodile, and the defeated French warships at the Battle of the Nile as exploding crocodiles. Napoleon himself became the 'Corsican crocodile dissolving the Council of Frogs' as he took control of France, gaping jaws signifying his appetite for power.[9]

Almost at the same time, Charles Darwin's grandfather Erasmus (1731–1802) penned an astonishing biological portrait of the development of a crocodile embryo, its growth analogous to its tidal habitat – presciently scientific, albeit poetically heightened:

So from his shell on Delta's showerless isle
Bursts into life the monster of the Nile:
First in translucent lymph with cobweb-threads
The brain's fine floating tissue swells, and spreads;
Nerve after nerve the glistening spine descends,
The red heart dances, the aorta bends;
Through each new gland the purple current glides,
New veins meandering drink the refluent tides;
Edge over edge expands the hardening scale,
And sheaths his slimy skin in silver mail.
– Erewhile, emerging from the brooding sand,
With tyger-paw he prints the brineless strand,

Peter Paul Rubens,
*Hippopotamus and
Crocodile Hunt*,
1616, oil on canvas.

High on the flood with speckled bosom swims,
Helm'd with broad tail, and oar'd with giant limbs;
Rolls his fierce eyeballs, clasps his iron claws,
And champs with gnashing teeth his massy jaws;
Old Nilus sighs along his cane-crown'd shores,
And swarthy Memphis trembles and adores.

The poem 'A Crocodile' by Thomas Lovell Beddoes similarly lies on the cusp of 'Orientalist' association, and naturalistic observation:

Hard by the lilied Nile I saw
A duskish river-dragon stretched along,
The brown habergeon of his limbs enamelled
With sanguine almandines and rainy pearl:
And on his back there lay a young one sleeping,
No bigger than a mouse; with eyes like beads,
And a small fragment of its speckled egg
Remaining on his harmless, pulpy snout;
A thing to laugh at, as it gaped to catch
The baulking, merry flies . . .

So by the nineteenth century, with imperial conquest well under way, both actual crocodiles and naturalists' more careful drawings and publications were spreading through public consciousness. As we have seen in previous chapters, imperialist Europeans regarded crocodilians everywhere as grotesque, unnervingly sneaky and formidable, and therefore as prime targets for their rapidly developing armaments. Hunters discovered in them a potent symbol of manly conquest, though one rarely encounters a genuine struggle, such as that depicted by Thomas Baines in 1856, allegedly of himself and 'C. Humphrey' despatching a giant

Australian 'alligator'. Almost always the 'battle' is conducted at that safe, not to say, cowardly distance enabled by the rifle – as in this 1850 account by Roualeyn Gordon-Cummings, one of the most rapacious of hunters in Africa:

> Presently, looking over the bank, I beheld three enormous crocodiles basking on the sand on the opposite side. I was astonished at their awful appearance and size, one of them appearing to me to be sixteen or eighteen feet in length, with a body as thick as that of an ox. On observing us they plunged into the dead water by the side of the stream. The next minute, one of them popping up his terrible head in the middle of the stream, I made a beautiful shot, and sent a ball through the middle of his brains . . .

This kind of account underpinned a flourishing of imperialist adventure fictions, too, such as those of G. A. Henty and H. Rider Haggard; in the latter's *The People of the Mist* (1884) a 'common Knobnose dwarf' is bizarrely pitched against a crocodile representing both 'the king of evil spirits' and the totem of the local tribe. Such imperial masculinist boasting soon came in for ridicule. Thomas de Quincey, in his infamous *Confessions of an Opium Eater* (1839), described a drug-induced dream, set in a suggestively Orientalist aura of both homoeroticism and bestiality, in which he was being 'kissed, with cancerous kisses, by crocodiles, and was laid, with all unutterable abortions, amongst reeds and Nilotic mud'.[10] More realistically, but with deliberately unmacho humour, inveterate traveller Mary Kingsley (rather luckier than Val Plumwood) beat off a crocodile attack in West Africa, when

> a mighty Silurian, as the *Daily Telegraph* would call him, chose to get his front paws over the stern of my canoe,

and endeavoured to improve our acquaintance. I had to retire to the bows, to keep the balance right, and fetch him a clip on the snout with a paddle, when he withdrew . . . This was only a pushing young creature who had not learnt manners.

In short, as Mary Leighton and Lisa Surridge suggest, the crocodile 'functions in many nineteenth-century texts simply to mark the frontier of otherness' and by extension 'the fear of colonial treachery, uprising or sneak attack – something lurking . . . almost invisibly under the surface of empire'.[11] This was true even of places where crocodiles did not occur, as at the Cape of Good Hope, where in 1819 George Cruikshank depicted the dangers of the frontier in juxtaposed images of 'Hottentot' and crocodile. (This would, nearly two centuries later, be parodied

Thomas Baines's painting of himself heroically despatch - ing an Australian crocodile, 1857, oil on canvas.

by artist Cyril Coetzee in an epic canvas for the Cullen Library at Wits, Johannesburg.) The sneak-attack motif – leavened perhaps by a sneaking admiration – was caught particularly memorably by Rudyard Kipling in his story 'The Undertakers' (1895), which is partly narrated by an Indian mugger: the crocodile recalls eating the bodies of sepoys, women and children killed in the 1857 Rebellion – but is shattered into three pieces by the elephant gun of a survivor 30 years later.

In 1859 Charles Darwin published *On the Origin of Species*, shaking up natural history, biology and philosophy for good. Scientific observation and the expansion of zoos, with conservation ethics closely following, would take increasing hold – though not, as we shall see, wholly displacing either moral repugnance or near-disastrous human destructiveness. On the other hand, parodic appearances of crocodiles if anything intensified, two particularly popular examples being Lewis Carroll's *Alice's Adventures in Wonderland* (1865) and J. M. Barrie's *Peter Pan* (1904). In the latter, the crocodile, having taken Captain Hook's hand, swallows both a clock and ultimately the yellow-blooded Captain himself. Even as it represents the conventional undertow of imperial violence, the crocodile is conflated with Hook; in Barrie's fantasy world, time is running out for Victorian conventions, and finally 'one stereotype consumes the other'.[12] As for Carroll, his little poem, which appears in *Alice's Adventures in Wonderland*, parodies hymnwriter Isaac Watts's pious Christian homily 'How doth the little busy bee / Improve each shining Hour':

How doth the little crocodile
Improve his shining tail,
And pour the waters of the Nile
On every shining scale . . .

Inadvertently parodic, finally, but symptomatic of the crocodile's pervasive presence in European literary culture, is the esoteric guru figure Madame Blavatsky (1831–1891). Charlatan though she undoubtedly was, Blavatsky was ferociously well-read in the world's occult texts, and her all-but-impenetrable discussion of the crocodile image exemplifies the (as it were) underwater channels by which crocodilian lore had spread. Blavatsky conceived (to summarize crudely) that human spiritual affairs are governed in astrological fashion by groupings of Celestial Beings, Creative Powers or *dhyanis*, powers which can be accessed through proper deployment of earthly symbols – a kind of intellectualized *vodun*. Intertwining several distinct traditions, here she discusses the Fifth group:

> In India and Egypt these Dhyanis were connected with the Crocodile, and their abode is in Capricornus. These are convertible terms in Indian astrology, as this (tenth) sign of the Zodiac is called *Makara*, loosely translated 'crocodile.' . . . In Egypt the defunct man – whose symbol is the pentagram or the five-pointed star . . . was shown emblematically transformed into a crocodile: Sebakh or Sevekh for 'seventh' . . . showing it as having been the type of intelligence [that] is a dragon in reality, not a crocodile . . . It is in Sekhem that lies 'the Mysterious Face', or the real man concealed under the false personality, the triple-crocodile of Egypt, the symbol of the higher Trinity or human Triad, *Atma, Buddhi* and *Manas*.[13]

Behind this quasi-mathematical tosh, one discerns the conventional crocodilian stereotypes lurking, and also something of the animistic mindset, worldwide and probably twenty millennia old, against which Western monotheistic and rationalist schema seem mere upstarts.

We divert finally to Europe's easternmost extension, hardly Europe at all: Russia. Russia is as unlikely a place as Japan to find crocodilia, but as early as 1865 Fyodor Dostoyevsky wrote his fanciful short story 'The Crocodile'. The story's main character is swallowed by a German-owned crocodile, representing anti-Russian cultural invasion. From its belly – made like a sack made of gutta-percha, and tellingly perfectly empty – he conducts a muffled conversation, the whole being an absurdist riff on Russia's dismal economics, science and the fickleness of journalism.[14]

In post-Revolutionary Soviet Russia, the crocodile seemed an appropriately subversive symbol for more than one satirical publication. *Krokodil*, a journal founded in Georgia in 1922, had limited licence to lampoon Russian politicians and institutions, but its main targets were Western capitalism, the Jews and anti-Marxist religions. Lasting until the collapse of the Soviet state, the magazine became itself a target of parody in composer Dmitri Shostakovich's *Five Romances on Texts from Krokodil Magazine* (1965). Beneath revolutionary politics, children's literature con-tinued to flourish. A grandfatherly favourite of many children was Korney Chukovsky (1882–1969) one of whose poetic 'Doctor Ayboli' stories projected a rather stereotypical depiction of a threatening Africa: 'Do not go to Africa for a walk! // In Africa, there are sharks, / In Africa, there are gorillas, / In Africa, there are large / Evil crocodiles / They will bite you, / Beat and offend you – '. Africa also contained the 'nasty, vicious, greedy Barmaley', a creature who in one of Chukovsky's stories then himself gets eaten by the crocodile – which, interestingly, is elsewhere related as eating the sun. This popular story and song was commemorated in the statue of the Barmaley Fountain, or Children's Khorovod, in Stalingrad, consisting of a group of children dancing around two snapping crocodiles. It was made particularly famous in photo-graphs by Emmanuil Evzerikhin, taken amidst the wreckage of

A 20th-century Russian book illustration of crocodilians.

the bombing of the city in the Second World War. The statue was restored, then removed in the 1950s, but nevertheless featured in several later films, including *Enemy at the Gates*, *V for Vendetta* and *A Clockwork Orange*.[15]

In perhaps the oddest manifestation of all – but one which foreshadows several of the themes of the next chapter – Krokodil

Gena is a friendly crocodile character in a series of Russian animated films, so popular he has been commemorated on a postage stamp. Gena works in a zoo, plays a kind of accordian called a garmon and sings. One of his songs contains the line, 'Such a pity that one's birthday happens only once a year', now a hugely popular birthday ditty. Watch Russian choirs singing it

A 20th-century Russian book illustration.

175

on YouTube – arguably the apotheosis of contemporary media. In today's globalized, electronic information marketplace, the multiple, contradictory manifestations of crocodilian presences and representations proliferate ever further.

9 The Contemporary Crocodile

Crocodilians and their lore had always spanned the globe but, in the massive expansion of travel and media accessibility in the twentieth and twenty-first centuries, their imageries range still more dramatically, from the familiar revulsion and fear through to the infantile and delusional, manifesting in every artistic and communicative medium imaginable. Here, I'll try to contain this proliferation within three broad areas: fictionalization, exploitation and conservation. If anything unites them, it is the sense that the crocodile still represents for most of humanity that which is deeply threatening and emotionally unreachable in the natural world – something like Sigmund Freud's notion of 'the uncanny'.

Written in 1919, Freud's influential psychoanalytic essay on the uncanny was prompted partly by a crocodile story, L. G. Moberly's 'Inexplicable', published in the *Strand Magazine* just two years before. In it, an English couple moving into a new house discover there an apparently abandoned, octagonal drawing-room table, whose top

> was a crust of carved leaves and flowers, and in each curve of the octagon there was a small alligator, his head point-ing outwards, his tail meeting the tails of the other croco-diles in the centre; and as the light fell on the scaly bodies they had an extraordinary look of life.[1]

Not only do these carvings seem to writhe and squirm, they are associated with a powerful, strange smell. This smell is explained (while simultaneously becoming even more inexplicable) by a guest, the traveller Jack Wilding, who with a start of 'cold fear' exclaims: 'I could have sworn I smelt that alligator swamp in New Guinea . . . It was dark, the place swarmed with those unspeakable devils; their stench was everywhere. It was dark – and poor old Danson – '. Danson, needless to say, had been eaten.

Freud is discussing the oral-sexual repressed underworld in human nature that he terms the 'uncanny', what he regarded as an 'infantile . . . over-accentuation of psychical reality in relation to material reality'. In critic Rod Giblett's view, the crocodile is also an image of the 'colonial repressed', something like the sense of threat we find articulated by Kipling and other Europeans abroad. At least part of the drive of contemporary and post-colonial treatments of crocodilians is to dislodge this creepy Freudian sense of its symbolic, half-concealed monstrosity. For example, a Brazilian novel, João Guimarães Rosa's *Grande Sertão: Veredas* (1956), seems to draw on Freud's notion of the crocodile as a symbol of the unconscious, but offers a counter to it, too. Far from being repressed, infantile and monstrous, Rosa's crocodile channels more positive powers of nature, acts as intermediary between worlds on the model of the Egyptian myths, and provides a psychological anchor in the novel's riverine world of perpetual flux. Far from wishing to eradicate the crocodile threat, or nullify it through psychoanalysis, Rosa's characters strive to become as crocodilian themselves as possible. Rosa elsewhere said:

I would like to be a crocodile in the San Francisco river. A crocodile is born or enters the world as the master of metaphysics, because for it every river is an ocean, a sea of wisdom, just as if it attained 100 years of age. I would like to be a crocodile because I like great rivers, because they are deep, like the soul of man.[2]

Between Rosa's 1956 work and Karen Russell's *Swamplandia!* (2010), I have found almost no adult novels which accord crocodiles anything more than stereotypical roles as passing threats. In some, like Bruno Schulz's collection *The Street of Crocodiles* (1933), Malaysian-born Beth Yahp's *The Crocodile Fury* (1993), Paul Hoffman's *The Wisdom of Crocodiles* (2000), and Lisa Moore's

A postcard illustrating 'Mr Punch and the Crocodile', late 19th–early 20th century.

Alligator (2010), the reptiles are little more than metaphors for human fears and desires. Mostly they lunge momentarily from swamps to eat people, and get despatched by the hero as he swings, like Tarzan, on to the next (usually colonialist) harum-scarum adventure. Only in the occasional short story do they become more central. In Edward Hoagland's brilliant story 'The Final Fate of the Alligators' (1992), the footloose protagonist agrees to look after a friend's New York apartment – complete with an alligator housed in a bathtub. At first the creature is chillingly daunting, 'a creature of barrel-like girth, with a rakish, pitiless mouth as long as a man's arm' and 'eel-grey' slitted eyes that 'seemed to have a light within them'. The owner never returns, the alligator grows, the increasingly hermit-like carer develops a certain intimacy,

Albino or leucistic crocodilians do not last long in the wild, but are great tourist attractions.

even fondness, but with a tragic inevitability the reptile expires in its tub: 'The expression was like the Angel of Death's, if, as seemed likely, an alligator confronts the Angel of Death with the expression of the Angel of Death.' He does not state it, but Hoagland indicates in his title that this particular alligator might be the last of its kind – and that much of nature might likewise die out, with not so much as a whimper, at the hands of uncaring or simply hapless human captors.[3]

Fictional crocodiles do appear frequently in children's books bearing titles like *The Cranky Crocodile, Crocodile Tears* and *See You Later, Alligator!* Maurice Sendak begins his children's alphabet with *Alligators All Around.* Most of these books entail a simplistic anthropomorphism which strips the crocodile of all threat. Arnold Lobel's 'The Crocodile in the Bedroom', for example, is a thoroughly sanitized version of Hoagland's sad captive; this croc finds the outside world altogether too bright and is comforted only by the wallpaper in his room. In Norman Catherine's *Legend of Memo the Hierophant* (1995), the alligator is the sewer-wise, limo-driving, heroic rescuer-of-situations. Popular South African storyteller Gcina Mhlope retails a sweet story entitled 'Crocodile, Tortoise and the Kind Man' (2007) in which the crocodile is associated with water, and after being helped by a boy in a drought-stricken land, magically brings the rain. This 'harmless' trend parallels the huge market for crocodile toys, from the small, rubbery and gaily coloured to the huge and inflatable. The educational and eco-conservation value of this imposition of innocuousness has to be deeply questionable. Fiction, in short, has not served the crocodilians particularly well.

Happily, there are innumerable educative children's books on crocodilians, and some quite brilliantly quirky ones, such as Emily Gravett's *The Odd Egg,* a winner of the Kate Greenaway Medal. Roald Dahl's well-known *The Enormous Crocodile* (1978),

Crocodiles as toys.

laced with his delightful signature cynicism, preserves something of the crocodile's intractable wildness. So, too, in a different way, does Alexander McCall Smith's Botswana-set story for young teens, *Akimbo and the Crocodile Man* (1993), in which a thoroughly modern conservation ethic balances understanding and preserving the crocodile with maintaining a respectful distance. Afrikaans poet Antjie Krog, in *Mankepank en ander monsters* (Mankepank and other monsters, 1985), more unsettlingly juxtaposes human belonging with ecological accuracy:

> who is the child
> with her arm around the crocodile
> who from his cruel teeth

peels nuggets and scraps of meat
see how she swims with him . . . [4]

Similar symbiosis happens in Indian writer Anushka Ravi-shankar's verse story, *Catch That Crocodile!* (2001), in which all efforts to capture a crocodile fail, until a small girl realizes that it's just lost and frightened, and calmly escorts it back to water. But this compassion is rare: more often, teeth are the focus, as in Shel Silverstein's poem 'The Crocodile's Toothache',[5] or the ending of the 'crocodile' entry in George Macbeth's poetic bestiary, 'Noah's Journey':

I would snap with a will. I have
toothache, though. Please, Noah, will you
give me a pill. In a mouth like mine
pain sprouts like a bush.[6]

Equally little educational accuracy characterizes another medium of contemporary fiction: the many pulp-horror films depicting crocodiles, which mostly infantilize their viewers. Perhaps the very earliest was Leon Benson's *Sea Hunt* (1958), in which the hero pursues an alligator escaped from a show into a Florida Lake. Tobe Hooper's *Eaten Alive* (1977) involves a Louisiana maniac feeding his victims to his African crocodile. *Alligator* (1980) was premised on the myth of baby alligators being flushed down the toilet; one, 'Ramon', grows huge in the sewers on the bodies of hormone-laced laboratory animals. Such films have proliferated into a numbing series of implausible bloodfests, including *Crocodile* (2000); *Death Swamp* (2001); *Primeval* (2007); *Lake Placid 1, 2* and *3* (1999, 2007, 2010); and *Black Water* (2007). *Lake Placid 2*, which involved, importantly, escaped African crocodiles, not nice patriotic American alligators, at least offered a solitary glimmer of humorous political critique: the unwise little old lady who had been feeding the monsters chicken bits had named one of them George – 'after the President [George W. Bush]. Because he's a bit *slow*, y'know'. Greg McLean's *Rogue* (2007), set in northern Australia, is somewhat better, despite its absurd underground-burrow denouement: the – inevitably – American hero kills the brute, a 'steam train with teeth', with a stake down its throat. The very notion of a 'rogue', however, is no more than a scapegoating projection of those primordial terrors, and the crocodile's demise a vicarious purging of them.

Documentary films have not escaped the lure of the melo-dramatic. The camera techniques have become increasingly dramatized by bewilderingly rapid cuts and zoom-ins, breathy voice-overs and portentous music. *Croc Ganglands* (2010), set in Zambia, is a case in point. Titles cater for the frisson-factor even when – as in the case of *Killer Crocs of Costa Rica* (2003) on Ameri-can crocodiles, or Caroline Brett's almost tender *Amazonia's Giant Jaws* (2007) on the black caiman – the content is relatively sober. Steve Irwin's *Crocodile Hunter* series, however educative, had much to do with stimulating a brand of documentary in which some swashbuckling 'naturalist' violently intrudes on the animals' lives and environment, ostensibly in pursuit of some esoteric bit of knowledge. Where one documentary dis-plays the macho, heavily whispering narrator dragging croco-diles bodily from their burrows, ostensibly to measure their length, Rom Whitaker's documentary for *National Geographic* similarly takes him around the world in search of 20-footers, but using perfectly simple and non-invasive methods of meas-urement. The dramatized genre reaches its peak – or nadir – in the u.s. television series *Gator 911* (2012), in which silly bravado, conservation ideals and animal welfare attain a particularly banal mix.

Here, fictionalization verges on, or merges into, exploitation. Some forms of exploitation may seem superficial, even benign, but arguably promote only prejudicial attitudes. For example, crocodilians lend their stereotyped qualities of shape and power to any number of human technologies. The first USS *Alligator* schooner-gunboat was commissioned in 1809 and served to protect the Carolinas coast in the war of 1812. The British man-o'-war *Crocodile*, commissioned in 1866, was deployed against slavers off the East African coast, and incorporated by Rider Haggard into his novel *Allan and the Holy Flower* (1915). A Swiss locomotive designed in 1922 to negotiate the steep grades of the St Gotthard tunnel was called the *Crocodile*. The LVT-4 Alligator landing-craft was used in the Second World War, including at Iwo Jima, and subsequently by the French in their 1950s Vietnam adventure Operation Carmargue. There was the Crocodile (colloquially 'Flat-dog') armoured troop-carrier of the Rhodesian war; the Alligator waterproof mackintosh of the 1950s; crocodile clips for electrical circuits; 'Gator' mechanical crushers; not to mention staplers and fridge magnets. So we are reminded of crocodilians even as they are simplified or sanitized.

Equally ambiguous is the colourfully hybrid world of advertising: consciousness of crocodilians may be raised and distanced

A crocodile jewellery 'box'; note the baby perched on the mother's back.

simultaneously. René Lacoste was Wimbledon tennis champion in 1925 and 1928, and was dubbed 'Crocodile' (in French *l'Alligator*) for his sporting tenacity, especially after the French Davis Cup captain had promised him a crocodile-skin suitcase if he won an important match. He began to sport a crocodile emblem on his blazers; this then attached itself to the line of more comfortable short-sleeved cotton piqué tennis shirts that Lacoste founded with André Gillier hosiery in 1933, pioneering the idea of sportswear as fashion. The crocodile logo, somewhat modified from its early versions, was further popularized in the 1970s, and is undoubtedly the most famous of its kind today, still prominent on Open Championship tennis courts. The Lacoste franchise has also gone on to market lines of crocodile-skin footwear, which it displays in conjunction with ruminations on the world's crocodilian myths; each shoe design is ostensibly inspired by appropriate national stories. Taking this yet a step further, Lacoste supports the Save Your Logo campaign, through which advertising revenue is hopefully channelled towards saving the actual creature on which your logo depends.

The relationship between commercial exploitation and conservation is a fraught one. Enterprises such as hunting, zoos and wildlife farming find it difficult even today to escape their grim historic debt to, and evolution from, capitalistic pillaging of the very resource they now desire to preserve. The line between hunting for fun and using the hunt to raise revenue for conservation is blurred. Many zoos are doubtless important to saving endangered species, and support good research, but always at a cost to individual animals' freedom and well-being. This is especially true in cases where zoos and 'parks' depend heavily on the animals' entertainment value to raise funds. Operations involving live crocodilians also still rely to varying degrees on the public's frisson at the strange and threatening. Some, like Gatorland in

Orlando, Florida, are primarily geared towards public entertainment through the deliberately comedic frenzy of feeding-time, the weirdness of their leucistic or albino specimens, and the voyeuristic thrill of 'wrestling', which is frankly abusive. Crocodile handlers everywhere like to pretend that turning a crocodilian upside down and tickling its tummy makes it relax into sleep; in fact, this motion interferes with the inner-ear mechanism and the animal blacks out. Thai entertainers seem particularly keen to stick their heads in crocodiles' mouths. Tickling the tongue is a favourite trick – and YouTube is replete with ugly footage of instances where this hubris has gone horribly wrong.

The size of the animal is everywhere played on, and the biggest can become story-book characters in their own right. The St Augustine Alligator Farm in Florida, for instance, devotes an extensive

Theme parks like to play with crocodilian terrors, as at this entrance in Oudtshoorn, South Africa.

display to 'Gomek', a saltwater crocodile from New Guinea who died measuring 5.4 m (17 ft-9 in). Originally named Louma Whalla Coremana Dikana by villagers on New Guinea's Fly River, the massive crocodile, having survived five decades including the Second World War, was finally captured by an Australian skin trader, George Craig. Renamed Gomek after a cartoon character, the poor creature lived a couple more decades on chickens and offal in Australian 'reptile parks' before relocation to the USA. St Augustine's have now replaced the deceased Gomek with another hefty saltie, 'Maximo'.

Exploitation peaks in the form of hunting crocodilians for skins, an industry which, as we have repeatedly seen, brought several species to the brink of extinction. Since the 1960s, crocodile farming has partially reversed the trend, though it is not always positive. At times, farming can be as damaging to wild populations as not farming at all. Technically, 'ranching', which sources stock from and replenishes wild populations, is good for conservation, but sometimes reality does not conform to theory. Most ironically of all, the IUCN's Crocodile Specialist Group, upon whose data much conservation depends, is almost wholly funded by leather industries.[7]

Probably crocodile skin has always been utilized by humans, from protective jerkins for warriors to applying it in powder form as an anaesthetic in the Middle Ages. Only with the advent of the European, firearm-wielding, imperial hunter in the eighteenth century, however, did such exploitation burgeon into a global industry. The macho pleasure of killing the despised and monstrous glutton quickly developed into wholesale slaughter to feed the luxurious appetites of Western and later Asian markets for shoes, handbags, belts, furniture and golf bags. Though Louis

Crocodile farming is now a multi-million-dollar global industry.

Vuitton introduced crocodile-skin travelling bags as early as 1892, uncontrolled hunting of wild crocodiles for their skins reached a peak between the 1940s and '60s. At that time it seemed to most hunters ethically unproblematic, indeed romantic and valorous. So Lawrence Earl could write in adventure mode in *Crocodile Fever* (1954) of one Bryan Dempster, who killed his first crocodile on the Zambezi at the age of eight and went on to the 'rewarding slaughter' of crocodiles for the skin trade, to the point of raffish illegality. By the early 1950s the Rhodesian government was curbing the overhunting of Zambezi crocodiles; Dempster and others were either retreating to still under-regulated Mozambique, or thinking of starting up farms. Amongst them was Bill Sutherland, whose adventures in the crocodile skin trade in the same region are related by Rory Macaulay in *Crocodile Trader* (1960). In this story, dramatized hunts are succeeded by the first attempts at live transport of crocodiles to England and the U.S., and the first crocodile farms. Never, however, does affection, or more than superficial understanding, intrude: 'to me', Sutherland relates, 'crocodiles are as repulsive and loathsome as snakes'.[8]

Hence in the 1960s, even as wild populations were perceived to crash, demand for crocodile-skin products and the growth of farming stimulated one another. Varieties of protective legislation began to take effect from the late 1960s onwards around the world. The 1966 Crocodile Trade Ordinance and the 1975 promulgation of CITES restrictions on wild captures and hunting, among other initiatives, necessitated a dramatic swing towards various farming possibilities. By 1986, one survey listed over 150 farms in 24 countries with a total crocodilian stock of 161,603. This involved not only breeding in captivity but, more disturbingly, 46,000 eggs and juveniles being removed from the wild. In the mid-1980s, up to 1.4 million skins were recorded as being traded out of over 30 countries.[9] The bulk of skins were caimans, and some two-thirds

Crocodiles are made into a vast variety of products, from belts made from their skins to preserved babies' heads.

came from captive-breeding operations. Market fluctuations aside, the skin trade appears robust.[10] A 2010 UN Environment Programme report on recorded skin transactions alone estimates an average of 1.3 million per annum between 1999 and 2008, with a peak of 1.8 million in 2006.[11] Just one crocodile-skin processing business, Zimbabwe's Padenga Holdings, who run three farms on Lake Kariba, reported a turnover of nearly U.S. $20 million in the 2010–11 financial year – and this despite economic near-meltdown in that country and a fall in demand during the 2008–9 global recession.[12] At the poorly documented consumer end, one leather-quality monitoring body lists and rates 213 suppliers and some 1,840 separate products,[13] but this must be only the tip of the iceberg. Illegal trade in skins, 'medicinal' parts and live animals also escapes accurate quantification; actual trade may be double the official figures, and detecting skins' true source is tricky. In one Bolivian case, the white preservative powder usually used on crocodile skins was replaced with cocaine: the same mafias traffic in both items. Even in relatively well-regulated northern Australia, poaching is allegedly depleting crocodile populations. The $15,000 tag on a large croc is just too tempting.[14]

Captive-breeding can also be controversial from an animal-rights viewpoint. Probably most farms try to adhere to legislated norms for humane rearing and harvesting procedures. Darwin Crocodile Farm in Darwin, Australia, for instance, advertises how hatchlings are raised in environmentally controlled pens and fed with vitamin-enriched mince, graduating to chicken heads until, at the age of three years or so, they reach an optimal belly width of 35–45 cm (13–18 in.). They are then electro-stunned, shot in the brain with a .22 bullet and the spinal cord pithed 'to minimize trauma', hung up to bleed, skinned, and the skins chilled and salted.[15] A Louisiana alligator farm calms the animals with music – they favour Cajun, apparently. Animal rights activists,

Alligator Breeders at Casper's Ostrich and Alligator Farm St. Augustine, Fla.

A rare postcard of an early Florida alligator farm, c. 1930.

however, assert that humane practices are frequently violated and short-cuts taken, to the extent of skinning the animals alive: 'It took an hour and 41 minutes for the alligator to die . . . held down to receive seven mighty blows on the back of the head, followed by a three-inch incision in the same spot to allow it to slowly bleed to death.' This to make a Louis Vuitton clutch-bag retailing for £3,820.[16] In addition, farmed crocodilians can contract (and inadvertently spread) sundry diseases, infections such as salmonella and dietary deficiencies; *Trichinella* parasites can carry from animal feed through crocodile flesh into humans.[17]

Public displays of crocodilian products has gone hand-in-hand with actually ingesting them: crocodile meat is sold worldwide today, averaging 400 tons annually though it constitutes a mere 1 per cent of the monetary value of crocodile trade. (I have sampled crocodile pie; it was fibrous and rather bland, and I didn't go back for seconds.) More lucrative is the trade in live reptiles for farm replenishment, zoos and circuses, and private ownership. Figures are elusive (and disputed), but according to one report at least 10,000 caimans were extracted from South

America in 2006 alone; and between 1999 and 2008 an alarming 286,000 were recorded exported from Mozambique, mostly to South Africa and Zimbabwe.[18] If even half true, the ecological impact of this scale of plunder can hardly be estimated. For private ownership, it is not difficult to buy one; caimans seem most popular. A baby *Palaeosuchus* will cost around us$500. A 1929 book touted the value of caimans as pets: 'fascinating' but still 'incorrigible biters' and 'the most vicious crocodilians imaginable'.[19] A spectacled-caiman owner in Kent, England, accordingly found his pet initially a 'nightmare', but now as 'good as gold'. He is just one of 72 registered crocodilian pets in England alone.[20] Keeping a pet crocodilian, especially in Europe, is a tricky business, involving, obviously, substantial supplies of water, food and courage, as well as precise temperature control. There are good reasons why it is illegal in Tennessee to keep an alligator in a bathtub. In truth, there seem to be few good reasons to keep a crocodilian at all.

Domestications of various shades, from the tens of thousands lying somnolently in skin-farms' concrete pens to solitary entrapments in private homes, have helped change at least some people's negative views of crocodilians. In the wild, though remaining a repulsive threat for the majority of folk, they have increasingly become an index of their ecosystems' health. This is partly because they are 'apex predators', and like lions or eagles indicate particularly sharply the viability of prey populations, and therefore of whole ecosystems. Because they consume such a variety of smaller species, they can also become vectors of concentration for toxins entering the environment, and suffer accordingly. Mercury and lead affect Everglades alligators; pesticides deplete broad-snouted caiman reproduction in Venezuela; heavy metals are found accumulated in the osteoderms of Australian freshwater crocodiles. A particularly intriguing case involved crocodiles on rivers in eastern South Africa. Despite the fact that they were 'safe' within the borders of the flagship Kruger National Park, in 2008 crocodiles began dying in alarming numbers – up to 500 that year alone. It transpired that the reptiles were contracting pansteatitis, a hardening of fat reserves which cramps mobility, and hence dying of exposure and starvation. The disease is contracted from

Crocodiles are still used medicinally worldwide, as here in a Bamako market, or in the West as 'croco-dillin' extract.

fish discarded by commercial operations, the die-off possibly exacerbated by toxins washing down from agricultural and mining operations.[21]

The situation can be summed up by a somewhat amusing, but revealing, anecdote. It involves a veterinarian, Gerhard, and some students, who were on a river netting fish in Kruger Park in search of such suspected toxins,

> when all of a sudden they noticed that along with the fish they had caught a large crocodile. Everyone panicked. The boat went rocking, and Gerhard pitched forward into the net. With the croc. Now, there was really no danger – the crocodile was more interested in getting away than biting anyone – until one of the male students in this tottering skiff pulled out a pistol he had secreted on his person and began blasting away in the general direction of the reptile. Both Gerhard and the croc immediately surrendered . . . The most dangerous thing by far in the Kruger is people walking around carrying guns.[22]

So crocodilians find themselves, for all their longevity and ubiquity, surprisingly vulnerable to the kinds of predation, exploitation and borderless environmental damage inflicted by an overwhelmingly larger human population – to the extent that they are being flagged as 'canaries in the mine' of global ecological decline. If they appear in contradictory ways, this is reflective of the contradictions in the human cultural psyche: the crocodilians are of course just being themselves. So crocodilians have not entirely lost their predatory fearfulness, especially in Africa and those shrinking regions where wild populations have retained or been restored to some health. Nor have they everywhere lost that reverential awe and symbolic force they once universally

John Drysdale's iconic photograph of the caiman as a pet, c. 1960s.

possessed under animist spiritual worldviews, against whose history and extent monotheism and scientific modernity are minority upstarts. Nevertheless, crocodilians have now widely been reduced to distant, even toy-like, status by global media and exploitative commerce. Efforts by those who try to conserve them as ecological treasures have not prevented half the world's crocodilian species becoming critically endangered; at the same time the modern sciences have gained us an unprecedented appreciation of the complexity, hardiness and uniqueness of this extraordinary reptile. One does not have to accept apocalyptic scenarios of humanity's demise to find it credible that, ultimately, the crocodiles might well outlive us.

Timeline of the Crocodile

250 million years ago	180 MYA	65 MYA	5 MYA
Bird and reptile evolutionary lineages diverge	First crocodiliforms appear	Crocodilians survive 'extinction event'	European crocodilians extinct

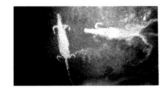

100 CE	c. 750	c. 1100	c. 1400	1530s
Pliny reinforces earlier crocodile misconceptions	Crocodiles carved in 'Sea of Milk' friezes at Angkor Wat	Medieval bestiaries equate crocodiles, dragons and the Devil	Caiman incorporated in Mayan-Aztec calendar systems	Crocodiles exhibited in early 'cabinets of curiosity'

1942	1950s	1963	1966
Japanese soldiers allegedly eaten by crocs on Ramree Island	Crocodilians decimated by hunting for skins	First Australian and Zimbabwean crocodile farms	Crocodile Trade Ordinance passed, regulating the crocodile skin trade.

| c. 7000 BCE | | 2000 BCE | 1000 BCE | 326 BCE |

c. 7000 BCE	2000 BCE	1000 BCE	326 BCE
Crocodiles appear in Australian Aboriginal rock art	Crocodilian motifs in Harappan script	Height of 'Sobek' worship in Egypt	Alexander the Great encounters crocodiles on the Indus

1791	1850	1892	1922
William Bartram encounters alligators in Florida	Morelet's crocodile discovered in Mexico	Louis Vuitton introduces crocodile-skin travelling bags	*Krokodil* satirical magazine founded in Russia

1975	1976	1988	2006
CITES restricts capture and hunting of crocodiles	Madras Crocodile Sanctuary established by Rom Whitaker	*Crocodile Dundee* filmed	Global skin transactions peak at 1.8 m

References

1 THE SURVIVOR

1 H. Stayt, *The Bavenda* (London, 1968), pp. 81–2.
2 R. Preece, *Brute Souls, Happy Beasts, and Evolution* (Vancouver, 2005), p. 284.
3 H. Harmon, *Tales Told near a Crocodile* (London, 1962), pp. 25–45.
4 S. Milius, 'Gator Feelings', *Science News*, 161 (18 May 2002), p. 310.
5 *Historia Animalium*, IX/6; trans. D'Arcy Wentworth Thompson (Oxford, 1910), p. 612.
6 G. M. Erikson et al., 'The Ontogeny of Bite-force Performance in American Alligator', *Journal of the Zoological Society of London*, 260 (2003), pp. 317–27.
7 D. A. Russell et al., 'At the Crocodilian Heart of the Matter', *Science*, 289 (8 September 2000), pp. 1687–8.
8 M. Merchant et al., 'Comparisons of Innate Immune Activity of All Known Living Crocodylian Species', *Comparative Biochemistry and Physiology*, 143 (2006), pp. 133–7.
9 S. Brito et al., 'Do Caimans Eat Fruit?', *Herpetological Natural History*, IX/1 (2002), pp. 95–6; J. Brueggen, 'Crocodilians Eating Their Vegetables', at www.alligatorfarm.com, accessed 17 July 2012.
10 H. Junod, *The Life of an African Tribe*, vol. II (London, 1927), p. 339.
11 G. Zug, 'Crocodilian Galloping: An Unique Gait for Reptiles', *Copeia*, 2 (1974), pp. 550–552.
12 K. Vliet, 'Social Displays of the American Alligator', *American Zoologist*, 29 (1989), p. 1019–31.

13 Oliver Wings, 'A Review of Gastrolith Functions', *Acta Palaeontologica Polonica*, LII/1 (2007), pp. 1–16.

14 L. Stejneger, 'Crocodilian Nomenclature', *Copeia*, 3 (15 October 1933), pp. 117–20.

15 E. Buffetaut, 'The Evolution of the Crocodiles', *Scientific American* (1979), pp. 130–144.

16 R. Broom, 'On Sphenosuchus and the Origin of the Crocodile', *Proceedings of the Zoological Society of London*, XCVII/2 (1927), pp. 359–70.

17 J. Wilson et al., 'New Crocodyliform (Reptilia, Mesoeucrocodylia) from the Upper Cretaceous Pab Formation of Vitakri, Balochistan (Pakistan)', *Contributions from the Museum of Paleontology, University of Michigan*, XXX/12 (2001), pp. 321–36; E. Buffetaut and Rucha Ingavat, *Scientific American* (1985), pp. 80–87.

18 S. Tarsitano et al., 'The Evolution of the Crocodilia: A Conflict Between Morphological and Biochemical Data', *American Zoologist*, 29 (1989), pp. 843–56.

19 H. Dessauer, 'Studies on the Molecular Evolution of the Crocodylia', *Journal of Experimental Zoology*, 294 (2002), pp. 302–11.

20 A. Janke and U. Arnason, 'The Complete Mitochondrial Genome of *Alligator mississippiensis* and the Separation between Recent Archosauria', *Molecular Biology and Evolution*, XIV/12 (1997), pp. 266–72.

21 K. Hirsch, 'Fossil Crocodilian Eggs from the Eocene of Colorado', *Journal of Paleontology*, LIX/3 (1985), pp. 531–42.

22 See E. Buffetaut, 'Evolution', in *Crocodiles and Alligators*, ed. C. Ross (London, 1989), pp. 26–41.

23 C. Brochu, 'Progress and Future Directions in Archosaur Phylogenetics', *Journal of Palaeontology*, LXXV/6 (2001), pp. 1185–1201.

24 P. Sereno et al., 'The Giant Crocodyliform *Sarcosuchus* from the Cretaceous of Africa', *Science*, 294 (2001), pp. 1516–19. 'SuperCroc', *National Geographic* (December 2001), pp. 84–9.

25 P. Booker, 'A New Candidate for Leviathan?', TJ (formerly *Technical Journal*), XIX/2 (2005), pp. 14–15.

26 'African-American Crocodiles', *Africa Geographic* (November 2011),
   p. 13.

2 NORTH AND WEST AFRICA

1 Figures throughout are derived from IUCN's Crocodile Specialist
   Group's most recent updates.
2 E. Yong, 'Nile Crocodile Found to Comprise Two Different
   Species', *Scientific American* (14 September 2011).
3 'TED Case Studies: Nile Crocodile Trade', at www.american.edu,
   accessed 17 July 2012.
4 G. Pinch, *Egyptian Myth: A Very Short Introduction* (Oxford, 2004),
   p. 40.
5 S. Quirke and J. Spenser, eds, *The British Museum Book of Ancient
   Egypt* (London, 1992), p. 133.
6 A. R. Williams, 'Animals Everlasting', *National Geographic*
   (November 2009), pp. 33–45.
7 'Graeco-Roman Papyrus Documents from Egypt', *Athena Review*,
   II/2, www.athenapub.com includes links to sites that reproduce
   and discuss papyri.
8 G. Maspero, *Popular Stories of Ancient Egypt*, trans. C.H.W. Jones
   (London, 1915), pp. 21–6.
9 G. Pinch, *Egyptian Mythology: A Guide to the Gods, Goddesses and
   Traditions of Ancient Egypt* (Oxford, 2002), p. 28.
10 Maspero, *Popular Stories of Ancient Egypt*, pp. 186–95.
11 C. G. Mann, ed., *Art of Ethiopia* (London, 2005). Catalogue by
   Arcadia Fletcher.
12 V. S. Naipaul, *Finding the Centre: Two Narratives* (London, 1984),
   p. 138.
13 Ibid., p. 133.
14 J. Reed and C. Wake, eds, *French African Verse* (London, 1972),
   pp. 12–13.
15 M. G. Anderson, *Ways of the Rivers* (Los Angeles, CA, 2002), p. 152.
16 S. P. Blier, *African Vodun: Art, Psychology and Power* (Chicago, IL,
   1995), p. 117.

17 Ibid., pp. 119, 163, 235, 238.

18 H. Drewal, *Sacred Waters* (Bloomington, IN, 2008), pp. 232–81.

19 Ibid., p. 351.

20 Ibid., pp. 125, 133.

3 CENTRAL AND SOUTHERN AFRICA

1 A. Graham, *Eyelids of Morning: The Mingled Destinies of Crocodiles and Men* (San Francisco, CA, 1990), pp. 21, 31, 32, 218.

2 'Gustave–Burundi's Killer Crocodile', BBC, www.bbc.co.uk (10 February 2010).

3 'After Eating 83 Villagers, Croc Beats Death Penalty', www.smh.com.au (14 March 2005).

4 D. Biebuyck, *Lega Culture* (Berkeley, CA, 1973), pp. 145, 215–17.

5 E. E. Evans-Pritchard, *Witchcraft, Oracles and Magic amongst the Azande* (Oxford, 1937), p. 484.

6 N. Isaacs, *Travels and Adventures in Eastern Africa* (London, 1936), vol. I, p. 161.

7 E. Holub, *Seven Years in South Africa* (Johannesburg, 1976), p. 236.

8 H. M. Stanley, *The Exploration Diaries of H. M. Stanley* (New York, 1961), p. 162.

9 D. Livingstone, *The Zambezi Expedition of 1853 to 1863*, ed. J.P.R Wallis (London, 1964), p. 65.

10 J. Stewart, *Zambezi Journal, 1862–1863*, ed. J.P.R. Wallis (London, 1952), pp. 73–5.

11 M. Gelfand, *Lakeside Pioneers* (Oxford, 1964), p. 301.

12 J.-A. McGregor, 'Crocodile Crimes: People Versus Wildlife and the Politics of Postcolonial Conservation on Lake Kariba, Zimbabwe', *Geoforum*, 36 (2005), pp. 353–69.

13 J. Appleby, ed., *Blue and Old Gold: A Selection of Stories from The Outpost* (Cape Town, n.d.).

14 E. Eastwood, *Capturing the Spoor: An Exploration of Southern African Rock Art* (Cape Town, 2006), p. 39.

15 T. Huffman, 'The Trance Hypothesis and the Rock Art of Zimbabwe', *South African Archaeological Society: Goodwin series*, vol. IV, pp. 49–53.

16 'Idi Amin: White House – State Department – NSC – CIA – British Government Files', at www.paperlessarchives.com, accessed 17 July 2012.

17 B. Freeth, *Mugabe and the White African* (Cape Town, 2011), pp. 64–70.

18 See also P. Godwin, 'Day of the Crocodile', *Vanity Fair* (September 2008).

19 H. Stayt, *The Bavenda* (London, 1968), p. 81.

20 P. Wilhelm, *The State We're In* (Johannesburg, 1999), pp. 31–2.

21 G. Mhlope, *A Book of Hope* (Cape Town, 1972), n.p.

4 SOUTH AMERICA

1 J. Thorbjarnarson and G. Hernandez, 'Recent Investigations of the Status and Distribution of the Orinoco Crocodile', *Biological Conservation*, 62 (1992), pp. 179–88.

2 G. Mourao et al., 'Aerial Surveys of Caiman . . . in the Pantanal Wetland of Brazil', *Biological Conservation*, 92 (2000), pp. 175–83.

3 Quoted by J. Thorbjarnarson, 'Secrets of the Flooded Forest', *Natural History* (March 2000), p. 1.

4 J. Thorbjarnarson, 'The Hunt for the Black Caiman of Brazil', *International Wildlife* (July 1999), p. 1.

5 B. de Thoisy et al., 'Genetic Structure, Population Dynamics, and Conservation of Black Caiman', *Biological Conservation*, 133 (2006), pp. 474–82.

6 J. Thorbjarnarson, 'Here Be Dragons', *Newsletter of the Madras Crocodile Bank Trust*, 3 (May 2008).

7 L. Kelly, *Crocodile: Evolution's Greatest Survivor* (Crow's Nest, NSW, 2006), p. 55.

8 A. Gray, *The Last Shaman* (New York, 1997), p. xi.

9 After Gray, ibid., pp. 83–5.

10 P. Descola, *The Spears of Twilight* (New York, 1993), p. 143.

11 Ibid., p. 324.

1 B. Helfgott Hyett, *The Tracks We Leave: Poems on Endangered Wildlife of North America* (Chicago, IL, 1996).

2 'Costa Rica's Crocodile Man, Tarzan Tico – Town of Sarapiqui', 7 October 2009, at www.ticotimes.com, accessed 6 November 2011. Pocho died in late 2009.

3 E.V. Pacheco and T. A. Ortiz, 'The Crocodile and the Cosmos: Itzamkanac, the Place of the Alligator's House', at www.famsi.org, accessed 17 July 2012.

4 C. J. Callemann, *The Mayan Calendar and the Transformation of Consciousness* (Rochester, NY, 2004), p. 240.

5 M. E. Smith. *The Aztecs* (London, 2003), p. 194.

6 Summarized after A. Campos, *Folktales of Mexico* (Tucson, AZ, 1977).

7 Cited in B. A. Botkin, *A Treasury of Southern Folklore* (New York, 1987), p. 489.

8 W. Bartram, *Travels through North and South Carolina, Georgia, East and West Florida* (Philadelphia, PA, 1791), p. 218.

9 B. J. Ancelet, ed., *Cajun and Creole Folktales* (Jackson, MS, 1994), pp. 161–2.

10 B. A. Botkin, ed., *A Treasury of Mississippi River Folklore* (New York, 1956), pp. 28–9.

11 P. Matthiessen, *Shadow Country* (New York, 2008), p. 37.

12 'Guessing the Alligators at the Charles Towne Landing', in *Alligator: Prehistoric Presence in the American Landscape*, ed. M. Strawn (Baltimore, MD, 1997), p. 25.

13 Animal Rights Foundation of Florida, 'Florida Alligators', at www.animalrightsflorida.org, accessed 17 July 2012.

14 See T. Craughwell, *Alligators in the Sewer, and 222 Other Urban Legends* (London, 1999).

15 S. Mirsky, 'What's Wrong with This Picture?', *Scientific American* (October 2003), p. 102.

16 At www.superheronation.com, accessed 9 December 2007.

1 H. Campbell et al., 'Estuarine Crocodiles Ride Surface Currents to Facilitate Long-distance Travel', *Journal of Animal Ecology*, LXXIX/5 (2010), pp. 955–64.

2 A. Britton, personal communication, 25 April 2012.

3 J. Flood, *Archaeology of the Dreamtime* (Honolulu, HI, 1988), p. 130.

4 R. and C. Berndt, *The World of the First Australians* (Chicago, IL, 1964), p. 332.

5 C. P. Mountford, *The Tiwi* (London, 1958), p. 26.

6 'Gumatjrom–Yolngu Art of Charlie Matjuwi Burarrwanga and Peter Datjin Burarrwanga', www.aboriginalartonline.com, accessed 22 November 2010.

7 L. Kelly, *Crocodile: Evolution's Greatest Survivor* (Crow's Nest, NSW, 2006), pp. 15–16.

8 C. Eden, *My Wife and I in Queensland* (London, 1872), pp. 294–5.

9 R. Reid, *Croc! Savage Tales from Australia: Wild Frontier* (Crow's Nest, NSW, 2008), pp. 83, 194.

10 M. Garlock, *Killer Gators and Crocs: Gruesome Encounters from across the Globe* (Guilford, CT, 2006), pp. 176–7.

11 *China Economic Net* (23 March 2007).

12 V. Plumwood, 'Human Vulnerability and the Experience of Being Prey', *Quadrant* (March 1995), p. 30.

13 Ibid., p. 33.

14 R. Giblett, 'Alligators, Crocodiles and the Monstrous Uncanny', *Continuum*, XX/3 (2006), pp. 299–312.

15 E. Stead, *The Gospel of Gods and Crocodiles* (St Lucia, Queensland, 2007), pp. 209, 91.

16 'Papua New Guninea Tribal Art', www.janeresture.com, accessed 4 December 2009.

17 J.-M. Cousteau, *Cousteau's Papua New Guinea Journey* (New York, 1989), pp. 152–5.

18 B. Allen, *Into the Crocodile Nest* (London, 1987), p. 183.

19 E. K. Silverman, 'Tourist Art as the Crafting of Identity in the

Sepik River', in *Unpacking Culture*, ed. R. B. Phillips and
C. B. Steiner (Berkeley, CA, 1999), pp. 51–66.
20 'The Crocodile Hunter: In Memoriam', at www.community.
discovery.com, accessed 17 June 2009.

7 ASIA

1 R. Aoki, 'A New Fossil Allocation of *Tomistoma machikanense*, a
Fossil Crocodilian from the Pleistocene of Japan', *Copeia*, 1 (1983)
pp. 89–95.
2 C. Pellegrino, *The Last Train from Hiroshima* (New York, 2010).
3 B. Wright, 'Battle of Ramree Island', at www.wikipedia.org,
accessed 17 July 2012.
4 *China Economic News* (16 January 2009).
5 *China Daily* (22 April 2007).
6 J. Thorbjarnarson et al., 'Wild Populations of Chinese Alligator
Approach Extinction', *Biological Conservation*, 103 (2002),
pp. 93–102.
7 'Surprise DNA Results Boost Chances of "Extinct" Crocodile',
at www.sapa.org.za, accessed 18 November 2009.
8 '2 Jailed for Beating Crocodile in Bangladesh', at www.sapa.org.za,
accessed 9 February 2010.
9 J. H. Lindsay, 'The Makara in Early Chinese Buddhist Sculpture',
Journal of the Royal Asiatic Society, 83 (1951), pp. 133–8.
10 Maung Htin Aung, 'Burmese Crocodile Tales', *Folklore*, XLII/1
(1931), pp. 79–82.
11 'Soldiers Hunt for Crocodiles Swept Away in Flood', *China Economic
Daily* (13 November 2007).
12 'Brunei Cops Hunt Killer Crocs', at www.sapa.org.za, accessed
12 November 2009.
13 'Captive Crocodiles Turn Predators,' *China Economic Net*
(25 June 2007).
14 J. Rodrigues, 'Goa's Unique Practice of Crocodile Worship',
Herald (20 January 2011), p. 1.
15 *Crocodile Specialist Group* newsletter, XXX/2 (2001), p. 21.

16 Adapted from Linda Brookover, 'The Gharial and the Monkey',
   at www.oneworldmagazine.org, accessed 17 July 2012.

17 W. A. Fairservis, 'The Script of the Indus Valley Civilization',
   Scientific American (1983), pp. 58–66.

8 EUROPE

1 H. M. Hubbell, 'Ptolemy's Zoo', *The Classical Journal*, XXXI/2
   (1935), pp. 68–76.

2 K. Edwards, 'Crocodile', *Milton Quarterly*, XXXIX/4 (2005),
   pp. 265–9.

3 W. B. McDaniel, 'A Fresco Featuring Pygmies', *American Journal of
   Archaeology*, XXXVI/3 (1932), pp. 260–271.

4 A. Miskimin, 'Britomart's Crocodile and the Legends of Chastity',
   Journal of English and Germanic Philology, LXXVII/1 (1978), pp. 17–36.

5 Ibid., p. 36.

6 A. Syme, 'Taboos', in *The Mark of the Beast*, ed. D. Hassig
   (New York, 2000), p. 167.

7 Edwards, 'Crocodile', p. 267.

8 P. Mauries, *Cabinets of Curiosities* (London, 2002).

9 M. L. Leighton and L. Surridge, 'The Empire Bites Back: The
   Racialized Crocodile of the Nineteenth Century', in *Victorian
   Animal Dreams*, ed. D. Morse and M. Danahay (Farnham, 2007),
   pp. 249–70.

10 Ibid., p. 261.

11 Ibid., pp. 254–5.

12 Ibid., p. 266.

13 H. P. Blavatsky, *The Secret Doctrine* (London, 1888), vol. I,
   pp. 219–20.

14 F. Dostoyevsky, *The Crocodile and Other Tales*, trans C. Garnett
   (Doylestown, PA, 2003).

15 'Barmaley Fountain', at www.wikipedia.org, accessed 17 July 2012.

1 Cited in R. Giblett, 'Alligators, Crocodiles and the Monstrous Uncanny', *Continuum*, 20/3 (2006), p. 303.

2 J. S. Dean, 'Upon These Banks and Shoals of Time: Herman Melville's Whale and João Guimarães Rosa's Crocodile', *Luso-Brazilian Review*, XX/2 (1983), p. 198. Author's translation, with Undine Weber.

3 E. Hoagland, *The Final Fate of the Alligators* (Santa Barbara, CA, 1992).

4 A. Krog, 'Krokodilikind' (Pretoria, 1985), p. 20. Author's translation, with Marike Beyers.

5 S. Silverstein, *Where the Sidewalk Ends* (New York, 2002), p. 66.

6 G. Macbeth, *Collected Poems, 1958–1970* (London, 1971), p. 132.

7 P. Brazaitis et al., 'The Caiman Trade', *Scientific American* (March 1998), p. 75.

8 R. Macauley, *Crocodile Trader* (London, 1960), p. 141.

9 R. A. Luxmore et al., *A Directory of Crocodilian Farming Operations*, IUCN (1986).

10 J. McGregor, *International Trade in Crocodilian Skins*, IUCN (2002).

11 J. Caldwell, *World Trade in Crocodilian Skins, 2006–2008* (UNEP, 2010).

12 *NewsDay* (18 March 2011); *Zimbabwe Independent* (23 September 2011), p. 5.

13 'Crocodile Skin Manufacturers and Crocodile Skin Suppliers', at www.globalsources.com, accessed 17 July 2012.

14 'Claims of Croc Poaching across the Top End', 19 April 2011, at www.abc.net.au, accessed 17 July 2012.

15 At www.4porosus.com.

16 Sue Reid, 'Getting Under their Skin', *Sunday Times* (16 February 1997), available at www.anapsid.org.

17 S. Pfitzer, '*Trichinella* Infection in the Nile Crocodile', *Hooo-Hooo* (2007), pp. 12–15.

18 Caldwell, *World Trade in Crocodilian Skins*, pp. 22–5. Richard Fergusson of the Crocodile Specialist Group, for one, regards these figures as misconceived.

19 Z. Vogel, *Reptile Life* (London, 1929).
20 J. Copping, 'Crocodile Is Living in a Bungalow in Kent', *Telegraph* (17 January 2010).
21 J. Myburgh, 'Nile Crocodile Die-off in the Kruger National Park', *Hooo-Hooo* (2009), pp. 16–17.
22 W. Gibbs, 'The Most Dangerous Animal', *Scientific American* (September 1995), p. 20.

Select Bibliography

Alderton, David, *Crocodiles and Alligators of the World*
    (New York, 1998)
Dostoyevsky, Fyodor, *The Crocodile and Other Tales*
    (Doylestown, PA, 2003)
Earl, Lawrence, *Crocodile Fever* (London, 1954)
Fougeirol, Louis, *Crocodiles* (Paris, 2008)
Garlock, Michael, *Killer Gators and Crocs* (Guilford, CT, 2006)
Graham, Alistair, *Eyelids of Morning: The Mingled Destinies of
    Crocodiles and Men* (San Francisco, CA, 1990)
Kelly, Lynne, *Crocodile: Evolution's Greatest Survivor*
    (Crow's Nest, NSW, 2006)
Levy, Charles, *Crocodiles and Alligators* (Secaucus, NJ, 1991)
Macaulay, Rory, *Crocodile Trader* (London, 1960)
McCarthy, Kevin, *Alligator Tales* (Sarasota, FL, 1998)
Reid, Robert, *Croc! Savage Tales from Australia's Wild Frontier*
    (Crows Nest, NSW, 2008)
Ross, Charles M., ed., *Crocodiles and Alligators* (London, 1989)
Stead, Elizabeth, *The Gospel of Gods and Crocodiles*
    (St Lucia, Australia, 2007)
Strawn, Martha, ed., *Alligator: Prehistoric Presence in the American
    Landscape* (Baltimore, MD, 1997)
Webb, G., and C. Manolis, *Crocodiles of Australia* (Sydney, 2009)

Associations and Websites

THE MABUWAYA FOUNDATION
Monitors conservation of the Philippine crocodile
www.mabuwaya.org

IUCN CROCODILE SPECIALIST GROUP
Provides annual newsletters, up-to-date reports and details across
all species
www.iucncsg.org

CROCODILIANS
Comprehensive and accessible site on crocodilian biology and status
www.crocodilian.com

ST AUGUSTINE ALLIGATOR FARM
Includes useful research and links
www.alligatorfarm.com

MADRAS CROCODILE SANCTUARY
Asia's primary crocodilian resource centre
www.madrascrocodilebank.org

FOR DETAILS OF CROCODILE-SKIN TRADE FIGURES
www.unep-wcmc.org
www.traffic.org/species-reports/traffic_species_reptiles28.pdf.
Includes IUCN updated information on species distributions, biology
and status

Acknowledgements

I knew little about crocodilians when I began researching for this book, and I am especially grateful to experts who generously corrected at least some of my more obvious errors. In some cases, where they disagreed with the sources I had consulted, I let my original stand, while trying better to flag those issues as contested. In particular, the following commented helpfully on all or parts of the manuscript: Adam Britton, John Brueggen of the St Augustine Alligator Farm, Richard Fergusson of the Crocodile Specialist Group and Rom Whitaker of the Madras Crocodile Sanctuary. Jonathan Burt at Reaktion Books also provided very useful critique.

Almost everyone I spoke to could offer some or other crocodilian story, source, artefact or picture, and I can neither remember them all nor include all their offerings in this short book, but the following especially helped supply materials, sources, ideas, critique, answers to queries, accommodation or moral support, and I thank them particularly: Peter Adams in Australia; Marike Beyers; Bob Bieder in Bloomington, Indiana; Billy de Klerk; Norbert Draeger; Martin Glover; Helen James; Simon Lewis in Charleston; Ben Maclennan; Gil Maghalaes de Neto in the Pantanal, Brazil; Simon Pooley; Rita Mesquita in Manaus; Anna Obazhaeva; Stephanie Pfenningwerth; Janet Pringle in Goa; Ann Smailes; Ryan, Kate and Sam Truscott; Malvern van Wyk Smith; Leigh Voigt; and my mother, Jill Wylie. Any number of libraries have, often unbeknownst to them, supplied information and leads, but the staff at the National English Literary Museum, Grahamstown, were especially helpful. My university, Rhodes University, Grahamstown, South Africa, and my colleagues at the Department of English generously granted me funding and time to pursue the project.

Photo Acknowledgements

The author and the publishers wish to express their thanks to the below sources of illustrative material and/or permission to reproduce it:

Author's collection: pp. 113, 193; Bigstock: p. 6 (Gautier Willaume); The British Library, London: p. 159; © Trustees of the British Museum, London: pp. 154, 157; John Drysdale: p. 197; photographed at the Palazzo Massimo venue of the National Museum of Rome by Mary Harrsch: p. 155; Istockphoto: p. 138 (Kayann Legg); Library of Congress, Washington, DC: pp. 11, 106; photo courtesy Gilbert de Maghalaes Neto: p. 87; Pinacoteca do Amazonas, Manaus, Brazil: p. 8; Rex Features: pp. 73 (Johan Opperman/Solent News), 76–9 (Design Pics Inc), 80 top (Sergio Pitamitz), 80 bottom (Nature Picture Library), 134 (Rob Maccoll/Newspix); Shutterstock: p. 10 (Dirk Freder); photo courtesy Paulo Silvio de Jesus da Silva, pantaindio@hotmail.com: p. 22; photo courtesy Malvern van Wyk Smith: p. 37; Werner Forman Archive: p. 30 (Euan Wingfield); Victoria & Albert Museum, London: pp. 142, 157, 179; photo courtesy Leigh Voigt: pp. 44, 45, 195; Dan Wylie: pp. 9, 13, 17, 20, 24, 33, 59, 63, 69, 71, 72, 82, 83, 84, 89, 90, 93, 95, 97, 104, 105, 112, 116, 117, 125, 126, 129, 130, 139, 140, 145, 146, 147, 180, 182, 185, 187, 188, 189, 191; Zoological Society of London: p. 163.

Index